Endless Joke: An Alternative Writing Manual
By David Antrobus

Acknowledgements

A big, awkward, sloppy kiss-ridden thank you to all the authors (you know who you are) at Indies Unlimited for their endless enthusiasm and infinite encouragement. And to every other writer who ever inspired me, which is far too long a list.

And another loud shoutout to Nancy Lee Parish for her excellent and sly work on the cover art. With apologies to the late genius, David Foster Wallace.

And finally, much love and gratitude for the inspiration and catalyst who made this collection possible, Monica Baguchinsky Lunn.

Table of Contents

Introduction

So what is this? And more to the point: why indeed should you read it?

Well, on the surface, it's a writer's manual, a handbook for the countless numbers of new authors currently trying to find a foothold in a brave new publishing world. But that only tells part of the story. It's also a satire of that world, a pastiche and a parody. While hopefully illuminating some of the scary pitfalls and honest-to-goodness pathways through the murky swamp of epublishing, it also pokes fun at it. All of it. Within these chapters, you will find writing tips and editing advice, much of it practical and yet simultaneously irreverent. It maps my own journey through that swamp, a journey that's far from over, and if on occasion it wails too loudly in frustration, perhaps it will be redeemed when it makes you laugh… and then makes you cry all over again. If, on occasion, I mock others too harshly, please recognize my self-deprecation, too. For every wagging finger of satire, after all, three others point back.

I don't pretend to define this book easily. Many of its chapters were originally blog posts for the web collective Indies Unlimited or for my own blog, The Migrant Type. I've tried to keep to a minimum the hyperlinks that were so tempting to preserve, since I personally don't surf the Web much on my Kindle, although it's possible that tablet users might.

Within these pages, you will encounter sinking ships, musings on soccer, tributes to literary greats and not-so-greats, punk rock, literary mashups, wordplay, shin-kicking contests, seahorse roe, Jersey Shore, urban legends, lists (oh, so many lists), beginnings and endings, poetry, social media, Joe Konrath, Dan Mader, Atticus Finch, Holden Caulfield, Yngwie Malmsteen, horror, movie magic, drunk sportswriters, Valley Girls, tricks, sonnets, meanness, strangeness, kindness, sorrow, rabid baboon esophagi, sparkly vampires, soccer moms, R. Kelly, Stephen King, fantasy, Lester Bangs, light spankings, Smashwords, pitfalls and cautionary tales, handicapped badger spleens, Canada, Heath Ledger, Kurt Cobain, Hannibal Lecter, Hunter S. Thompson, Shakespeare, zombies and Wu Tang Clan. Although, sadly, no nudity.

Yes, you might recognize the cover photo and even the title. It seemed fitting to me that, in a book filled with satire, mockery, self-loathing and pastiche, the very cover should be laden with poorly thought out gags, horribly embarrassing, misplaced hubris and other fun stuff… Not least, the title of the book itself, which is very much a parody of a tribute to a dead man. In my case, a cloth-eared, bathetic caricature of David Foster Wallace's *Infinite Jest*, the title of which is, in turn, a paean to Shakespeare himself:

Hamlet: "Alas, poor Yorick! I knew him, Horatio, a fellow of infinite jest, of most excellent fancy." (*Hamlet Act 5, scene 1*)

In keeping with many of the essays here, I am caught in a web of my own making. Tracing a lineage from Shakespeare to Wallace to…. well, *me* makes a mockery of the very idea of lineages in the first place. And don't forget, a joke you have to explain is no longer much of a joke. Sigh.

Okay, by now, you will have gotten the idea. Read these essays and articles any way you choose: for writing advice (and there is plenty of that, you might be surprised to know); for a trench-level perspective of the publishing wars; for the often jumbled, sometimes anguished and occasionally lyrical thoughts of a writer who has loved the power and the beauty of words for longer than he wishes to remember. If it helps you learn some practical stuff about said words, that's all well and good; if it allows you to remain in love with their beauty and power, even better.

Here there be tygers, sure: some of them may roar, some of them even bite, but many of them will smile and purr and only want to be your friend.

Chapter One: A Titanic Struggle

This will be a short rant, and if you think that's a contradiction in terms, or you're not in the mood for another soapbox oration, then fair play to you, but Imma do it anyway (and if you dislike the word "Imma", please know I feel your pain).

Briefly, and to state the fairly obvious to anyone paying attention to this topic, the sleek luxury liner world of writing and publishing has been impacted and upended by the hidden iceberg of new media and the digital revolution. The Titanic-like so-called Big Six publishing houses broke apart and are still slowly sinking as we speak, perhaps to be reconstituted at a later date. After some early and notable successes with epublishing, a gathering tide of new independent authors grabbed onto the flotsam and jetsam and headed for shore. It was and continues to be a dangerous but exhilarating journey.

Now, before its apparent demise, this Titanic was able to blast its horn on a global scale and nobody minded. It had impeccable staff and gatekeepers, directing authors and readers to their appropriate areas and even providing personal grooming (editing) and advocacy (marketing) services for the former. But now, without them, the individual authors doggie-paddling desperately in the icy waters must resort instead to scrawled messages on pieces of debris: "help me!" "don't let me drown!" "please read this!"

So, here we are. Many of those independent writers desperately trying to reach the shore, some having made it and dried off and been fed hot soup, but most still in the pitiless ocean, continue to need help if they are to survive. And yet, there are those who would deny them their right to call attention to themselves for reasons of what has come to be known as "shameless self-promotion".

Flawed analogies aside, what prompted this little outburst on my part is this idea that when a great number of small people promote their work, much of which is born of pain and sweat and long, dark nights of the soul—you know, work, right?—it is referred to as "spam" or even "gaming the system", yet when the sleek ocean liners of the world do it on a grand, monstrous scale, it's referred to as "advertising". Once again, why does the bulk of the moral opprobrium descend like freezing rain on the tiny, far more desperate swimmers and rarely on the monolithic giants? Because it's easier to pick on them? Safer? Have we really become such cowards?

Anyway, with more and more writers in sight of shore, clutching their makeshift signs and shivering in the dark, I worry about what we will do next—welcome them home or push them back out in the frigid waters?

Chapter Two: Punk Fire or Indie Schmindie

Inspired by an excellent post by fellow traveller Dan Mader, I've been doing some thinking about what it means to be an indie author in relation to this new publishing milieu within which we find ourselves.

On numerous occasions, Dan and I have discussed the parallels with the punk rock movement of the late 1970s (in the UK and in New York) and beyond (post-punk in the UK, hardcore and straight edge in the United States) leading to "alternative" music in the '90s. And they are indeed striking; with the long tail of minimally talented yet enthusiastically raw artists, the do-it-yourself improvisation, unrealistic expectations and the overall lack of financial success, the slightly dodgy/murky concept of not selling out, of "authenticity", even the sense that the rough-hewn fanzines of old have been replaced by blogs... all of which has contributed to a sense of déjà vu for anyone who has been steeped in both cultures particularly.

But here is something else. If you extend the history of punk and conflate it (perhaps somewhat unfairly, although a case can certainly be made) with the musical genre known ominously as "indie", things are perhaps not so cut and dried. Indie as it was once identified, particularly in the UK in the '80s, referred to music that was not signed to a major label, literally to an independent label. And with innovative labels such as Factory, 4AD, and Creation, the music was rich, inventive and became a genuine alternative to the more "mainstream" rock and pop of the day. But something else happened. Soon, the term "indie" was being applied to a style of music and not to the commercial environs of the labels themselves. Mostly rooted in post-punk, it made its way across the Atlantic until, today, indie is a full-fledged genre unto itself... although here lies the problem. It's kind of stale. It's kind of rhythmically-challenged. It's kind of snobby. It's kind of soulless... or precious... or, worse, one-dimensional and gutless. So much so that some have taken to calling it "indie-schmindie" to denote a very marginalized, very vanilla, very bland type of prettified ephemera.

So, here's the dilemma. If you even partially agree with my somewhat broad and no-doubt slightly unfair characterizations above, you might begin to worry about how it may all play out for indie authors. We're still at the punk rock stage, in which the initial euphoria and electric uncertainty of everyone being a producer and not merely a consumer is still palpable. A buzzing awareness of possibilities. Some dream of making it big, of being the Clash, if you will. Others just enjoy the sense of belonging while hoping to find the right audience. Now, Dan's post and my own sentiments fall neatly into the latter camp. Making it big is still a lottery. Playing for others, then returning the favour the very next night by showing up and watching those same folks don their metaphorical Strat copies and studded, zippered bondage pants, is the fun part... but where will it end? If it ends all stunted and ghettoized while the same tiny minority make off with pretty much all the pie, we'll have failed, no matter how much fun we may have had for a time. Preaching to the choir, writing only for other writers, however much it can be a blast, may be a *good* look but is not a sustainable one.

Epublishing should be a great leveler. The problem with that is nothing *stays* level, not for long. And in some ways, that's okay. A great many bands played to ten or fifteen friends in their garage and were pretty fucking awful, and so let's be honest here: many indie writers can't actually *write*, which is a pretty big handicap when you come right down to it. But where does that leave those of us with some degree of talent? Can the market sustain a Clash and a Pistols (Konrath, Eisler?) while also maintaining some level of success for the Slits and Wire and Gang of Four and UK Subs, not to mention the tens of thousands of equally worthy yet far lesser-known artists still?

The danger is, we'll be drowned in an oversaturated market in which everyone and his or her dog believes the gravy train is pulling into the station. Okay, excruciating mixed metaphors aside, it's all very well buying into a new and exciting landscape of DIY innovation, but if we descend into a future of mediocrity amid an environment in which the Amazons/Apples of the world simply replace the often exploitive practices of the Big Six publishing houses, and only a tiny handful of artists grow rich, what will we have gained? A sense of fun and camaraderie at the expense of a career. Because, really, why can't good writers plough those talents and that energy into an actual career? Why do they, or we, not deserve that?

None of which is a criticism of those very aspects which inspired this post. Like Dan, I am grateful to be surrounded by such positive and talented people, who often give of themselves for the pure joy of paying it forward and helping their peers. I simply hope that each and every one of them finds some reward over and above the satisfaction of belonging to a community, rich as that can be in and of itself.

I suspect fire in the belly—the fervor of innovation, the ardor of love—will be key ingredients in that goal.

Chapter Three: Breaking the Rules

As much as we sometimes pretend we don't, we love rules. Even the most maverick of writers is receptive to those clever, memorable guidelines, if only to know what to kick against. And the reality is that rules for writing—as for life, let's face it—are not only abundant but are bewilderingly contradictory.

See, the thing about rules for writing is that, kind of like a yin-yang symbol, they always contain cute little seeds of their exact opposites. Witness the exhortations—from such authoritative guides as Strunk & White's *The Elements of Style* and George Orwell's *Politics and the English Language*—to err on the side of simplicity, to avoid in particular the pretensions of Latin- and Greek-based language in favour of good old Anglo-Saxon English (put simply and memorably: "avoid fancy words"). Plain common sense advice about plain common sense English, right? Well, yes and no. Outside the secret and no-doubt sordid fantasies of botanists everywhere, Orwell's example of a *snapdragon* is still in no danger of being superseded by *antirrhinum* almost seventy years after he expressed his reservations. Similarly, *ameliorate* and *clandestine* have their place, even if we are more often inclined to use *help* and *secret*.

The thing is, contained within this particular dictum is a received wisdom that is equally worth challenging: that pretension is somehow wrong or unseemly.

Personally, I'd trust a style guide that said something along these lines: "if your intuition (sorry, 'gut' if you love the Anglo-Saxonisms) tells you that what you're currently writing requires some pretension, then don't shy away from it". The music of the Ramones was every bit as much a product of artifice as anything produced by Van der Graaf Generator. And there may well be moments during your writing (for pacing, for rhythmic or melodic reasons) that require the risk of spouting the dreaded purple prose. In which case, I say go for it. Life is risk. Hell, *writing* is risk. Let the rules take a back seat once in a while. After all, playing soccer in just the penalty area is called "training"; you use the whole field when you play the actual game. Or, more in keeping with my tortured metaphor, that guitar you coveted and saved for and so proudly brought home in its sleek black case happens to have six strings and twenty frets, so why only noodle around on the top E string and the lower three frets every time? You didn't buy it just to stroke its feminine curves, did you? (Please don't answer that.) And I haven't even started on effects pedals...

I'm not saying go all Yngwie Malmsteen here—a sweaty blur, shredding 'til your fingers bleed, hands like demented octopi—but the odd flourish might not go amiss. Of course, you're not Jimi or Jimmy and your attempts will probably fall flat, but what if by reaching, by risking *over*reaching, you unveil something in your style you weren't previously aware of, a capacity for lyricism or poetry, a music previously unsung? I'd say that's worth the risk, wouldn't you? Especially since, by baring our souls so publicly, we're already making complete fools out of ourselves anyway.

Chapter Four: The Three Rs - Rules of Riting Revisited

So, after flirting with rebellion in that last chapter, I'm now going to continue to obsess about rules, just like that lady who didth protest too much.

In my defence, rules are kind of fascinating, even when we disagree with them. I mean, how was it decided, for example, that in the English city of Chester, you can only shoot a Welsh person with a bow and arrow inside the city walls after midnight? Not even sure which part of that rule I disagree with most, especially since it's apparently okay to shoot a Scotsman with a bow and arrow in York at any time of day or night. Except Sundays. (Oh, that's alright, then. And no, I promise I'm not making any of this up, you can check.)

But, back on track. My purposes here are to highlight a really cool link, in which the *Guardian* newspaper, following an excellent response by crime writer Elmore Leonard to a similar request, asked a bunch of accomplished writers to list up to ten "rules of writing" of their own. It really is an impressive list. Now, I could simply point you there and hope you go read them, in which case this would this be a very short blog post, but the piece itself is very long, is in two parts, and honestly, even I am not that naive. So instead, I'll grab a fairly random handful of these rules, and hold them up for inspection. As well as mockery. Okay, not mockery; some sporadic light teasing, perhaps. All done in a spirit of affection, of course.

1. Elmore Leonard: "If it sounds like writing, I rewrite it."

Hey, Elmore, that sounds a bit like writing to me. What's that? Uh. Just kidding.

2. Margaret Atwood: "Take a pencil to write with on aeroplanes. Pens leak. But if the pencil breaks, you can't sharpen it on the plane, because you can't take knives with you. Therefore: take two pencils."

I now have an unrequited urge to ask the redoubtable Ms. Atwood if she's heard of pencil sharpeners. Or mechanical pencils. Or, uh, iPads.

3. Geoff Dyer: "Have regrets. They are fuel. On the page they flare into desire."

Uh-huh. Nodding my head vigorously if slightly stupidly here. Okay, not a good look. Moving on.

4. Ann Enright: "The first 12 years are the worst."

Yes. And I would add—in flagrant violation of the entire principle of comparatives versus superlatives—that the next 12 years are also the worst. Face it, it never gets better. And I don't even think I'm kidding this time.

5. Ann Enright: "Only bad writers think that their work is really good."

I must like short and punchy, since Ms. Enright gets two entries in a row here. And yes, I included this because we all feel hubris sometimes—until hubris grows suddenly weary of being felt and makes a break for it, leaving us alone with our far more familiar companion:

crippling self-doubt. Screw you, hubris, we never loved you anyway. Sob.

6. Richard Ford: "Try to think of others' good luck as encouragement to yourself."

Good man! The spirit of Indies Unlimited right there. I also enjoy that he follows it up with "Don't take any shit if you can possibly help it," which achieves a certain balance between gracious and curmudgeonly, one of the more difficult poses to maintain, I've found.

7. Esther Freud: "Trust your reader. Not everything needs to be explained. If you really know something, and breathe life into it, they'll know it too."

Leave a little mystery, let your readers fill in the gaps. This feels like all-round good advice, like when the Brazilian government encouraged people to pee in the shower.

8. Neil Gaiman: "Write."

Well, thanks for that, Neil. Must have scratched your noggin a good while before coming up with that one. But wait, hold up, he's not done. He follows up later— like a drunk sportswriter mixing metaphors—with a slam dunk out of left field right in the top corner…

9. Neil Gaiman: "Remember: when people tell you something's wrong or doesn't work for them, they are almost always right. When they tell you exactly what they *think* is wrong and how to fix it, they are almost always wrong."

I take from this: listen to the instincts of others—at first—but be wary if they then try to help you write the specific story *they* want to read, and not the story *you* want to read. Kind of like that initially harmless and even amusing drunk who then proceeds to follow you home from the bar. The one you turn to at some point, growl at in a low yet threatening voice to go write his own story and stop creeping yours. Sure, the metaphor died a little there, but what of it?

10. P. D. James: "Write what you need to write, not what is currently popular or what you think will sell."

This. Thank you. More of us need to pass this on. And very much related is Hilary Mantel's "Write a book you'd like to read. If you wouldn't read it, why would anybody else? Don't write for a perceived audience or market. It may well have vanished by the time your book's ready." In other words, drop those sparkly-vampire boy-wizards now, you don't know where they've been. (Actually, a better observation would be that you *do* know where they've been.)

11. Andrew Motion: "Think with your senses as well as your brain."

Again, succinct. But an invitation to live inside your story, to translate the sights, smells, sounds and textures into words. The real magic of writing. Maybe it takes a poet. And yes, that was an entirely sincere one.

12. Will Self: "You know that sickening feeling of inadequacy and over-exposure you feel when you look upon your own empurpled prose? Relax into the awareness that this ghastly sensation will never, ever leave you, no matter how successful and publicly lauded you become. It is intrinsic to the real business of writing and should be cherished."

I sense some disturbing similarities between writing and sex here. Perhaps brought on by the slightly disquieting word "empurpled". We could investigate further. Or we could succumb to a probably fortuitous hybrid of wisdom and cowardice and move on…

13. Will Self: "The writing life is essentially one of solitary confinement – if you can't deal with this you needn't apply."

14. Will Self: "Oh, and not forgetting the occasional beating administered by the sadistic guards of the imagination."

15. Zadie Smith: "Tell the truth through whichever veil comes to hand – but tell it. Resign yourself to the lifelong sadness that comes from never being satisfied."

A basic density being my default mode, even *I'm* beginning to pick up from the last few examples that writing is probably not the ideal pursuit if your goal in life is, uh, to be happy. Damn. Hmmm. It really is too late, isn't it?

16. Sarah Waters: "Talent trumps all. If you're a really great writer, none of these rules need apply. If James Baldwin had felt the need to whip up the pace a bit, he could never have achieved the extended lyrical intensity of *Giovanni's Room*. Without 'overwritten' prose, we would have none of the linguistic exuberance of a Dickens or an Angela Carter. If everyone was economical with their characters, there would be no *Wolf Hall* . . . For the rest of us, however, rules remain important. And, crucially, only by understanding what they're for and how they work can you begin to experiment with breaking them."

Aside from a dodgy subject-verb issue, this comes closest to saying what I've been trying to express in my last two posts. It encapsulates that ambivalence with eloquence (ouch, after that particular ornate string of Latinate pretension, I will now be hounded for life by the finger-wagging ghost of William Strunk). But it does. And I would argue that the last clause, encouraging as it does the possibilities inherent in such experiments, may lead a few of us toward that greatness… or at the very least to soar awhile in that rarefied air. While waiting for the inevitable plummet earthwards, no doubt, toward a horribly gruesome crash that will nonetheless have been well earned.

And finally, if only because it's both funny and annoyingly smartass to point out a paradox, here's the ultimate (non) rule…

17. Michael Moorcock: "Ignore all proffered rules and create your own, suitable for what you want to say."

(Seventeen? What kind of number is that? Who makes lists of *seventeen?* And yes, I did completely make up the word "didth" back there.)

Chapter Five: Ten Endings

I want to talk about endings. How important they are, obviously; but more because I simply want to share some of my favourites. A lazy chapter, in a way, but perhaps a fun or enjoyable one nonetheless. I love a well-crafted passage of writing, wherever it occurs in a book, and most who love language would probably concur. Yet more satisfying and occasionally beautiful still are those final lines of a novel that both summon and summarize the themes and rhythms of the entire narrative in a handful of incredibly wrought, startling, sorrowful exquisite, elegiac sentences.

Some quotes stand alone, gorgeous synecdoches (oh, come on, you have a dictionary); others require the full context of the preceding novel. No matter. Beauty is beauty, and in my own writing I use these as perhaps unattainable benchmarks for how I want my language to develop and move throughout a piece. I say unattainable, because for me a sublime failure is still more interesting than a bland success. If I had written anything even approaching the brilliance of any of these, I might just retire happy… or not. Yeah, probably not. I offer these without commentary or void even of my usual lame attempts at humour. Savour them and please consider your own favourites while doing so.

(It ought to go without saying, really, but this is some mad spoiler territory.)

1. "Don't ever tell anybody anything. If you do, you start missing everybody." — J.D. Salinger, *The Catcher in the Rye*

2. "Then there are more and more endings: the sixth, the 53rd, the 131st, the 9,435th ending, endings going faster and faster, more and more endings, faster and faster until this book is having 186,000 endings per second." — Richard Brautigan, *A Confederate General from Big Sur*

3. "Everything had gone right with me since he had died, but how I wished there existed someone to whom I could say that I was sorry." — Graham Greene, *The Quiet American*

4. "We were alone with the quiet day, and his little heart, dispossessed, had stopped." — Henry James, *The Turn of the Screw*

5. "He fits himself around her, her silk pyjamas, her scent, her warmth, her beloved form, and draws closer to her. Blindly, he kisses her nape. There's always this, is one of his remaining thoughts. And then: there's only this. And at last, faintly, falling: this day's over." — Ian McEwan, *Saturday*

6. "Listen. Slide the weight from your shoulders and move forward. You are afraid you might forget, but you never will. You will forgive and remember. Think of the vine that curls from the small square plot that was once my heart. That is the only marker you need. Move on. Walk forward into the light." — Barbara Kingsolver, *The Poisonwood Bible*

7. "So in America when the sun goes down and I sit on the old broken-down river pier watching the long, long skies over New Jersey and sense all that raw land that rolls in one unbelievable huge bulge over to the West Coast, and all that road going, all the people dreaming in the immensity of it, and in Iowa I know by now the children must be crying in the land where they let the children cry, and tonight the stars'll be out, and don't you know that God is Pooh Bear? the evening star must be drooping and shedding her sparkler dims on the prairie, which is just before the coming of complete night that blesses the earth, darkens all rivers, cups the peaks and folds the final shore in, and nobody, nobody knows what's going to happen to anybody besides the forlorn rags of growing old, I think of Dean Moriarty, I even think of Old Dean Moriarty the father we never found, I think of Dean Moriarty." — Jack Kerouac, *On The Road*

8. "I lingered round them, under that benign sky; watched the moths fluttering among the heath, and hare-bells; listened to the soft wind breathing through the grass; and wondered how anyone could ever imagine unquiet slumbers for the sleepers in that quiet earth." — Emily Brontë, *Wuthering Heights*

9. "Hill House itself, not sane, stood by itself against its hills, holding darkness within; it had stood so for eighty years and might stand for eighty more. Within, walls continued upright, bricks met neatly, floors were firm, and doors were sensibly shut; silence lay steadily against the wood and stone of Hill House, and whatever walked there, walked alone." — Shirley Jackson, *The Haunting of Hill House*

10. "It had ceased raining in the night and he walked out on the road and called for the dog. He called and called. Standing in that inexplicable darkness. Where there was no sound anywhere save only the wind. After a while he sat in the road. He took off his hat and placed it on the tarmac before him and he bowed his head and held his face in his hands and wept. He sat there for a long time and after a while the east did gray and after a while the right and godmade sun did rise, once again, for all and without distinction." — Cormac McCarthy, *The Crossing*

Chapter Six: Found Words, Waiting

I was thinking about how writing dovetails with our wider lives, the lives we may lead outside the tiny cramped space in which we sit for hours hunched over a screen that slowly eats the cones and rods from within our dark-shadowed eyes, perhaps even the sanity from behind our knitted brows, lost amid a precarious landscape built from stacked pizza boxes and empty wine bottles and other far less wholesome things. You know… that place outside we call "the world"? I ventured into my corner of it recently (Vancouver, British Columbia) and even there I began to notice the marks and stamps left by other writers. Either that or I'm now so delusionally obsessed with writing I've reached the point of developing a serious pathology.

Vancouver's most acclaimed literary figure was probably Malcolm Lowry, who wrote *Under the Volcano* here. William Gibson, Evelyn Lau and Douglas Coupland also spring to mind. But I don't really mean that. I'm not so much interested in the indisputably famous and lauded, but more the quieter language moments we sometimes stumble on by accident.

A case in point is the Fairmont Pacific Rim Hotel in downtown Vancouver. If you are ever in town, it's an otherwise fairly nondescript piece of modern architecture (think steel, concrete and green-tinted glass) at the intersection of Burrard and Cordova, but what makes it remarkable is that a one-line poem wraps around 17 stories of its facade. Written by British artist Liam Gillick, it reads:

"lying on top of a building the clouds looked no nearer than when I was lying on the street"

Understated and minimalist, its impact undoubtedly dependent upon its being experienced in context, it nevertheless offers a patina of beauty to an otherwise ordinary late winter day in the city; a reminder that language, as abstract as we sometimes suppose, can also be such a visual and visceral thing of the world.

And that isn't all. I found myself at the main central library and once again, even before entering what is frankly a stunning building in its own right, more understated words introduced themselves to me like slightly reticent predators.

THE WORDS DON'T FIT THE PICTURE

Which is artist Ron Terada's poetic expression of Vancouver's historic relationship with bright, neon signs. Or as he puts it himself: "The sign takes its cues from an era of signage when signs were seen as celebratory, grand and iconic – in effect, as landmarks in their own right, a kind of symbolic architecture… Taken within the context of a public library, the work touches upon – in a very poetic way – the use of words and language as boundless and imaginative, as a catalyst for a multiplicity of meanings."

And still we weren't done, because inside the breathtaking atrium, there were yet more words, way up on the precipitous walls. Mysterious and, again, quietly poetic words. This time, it required some detective work to discover their source, detective work that hasn't paid off at the time of writing (if my inquiries pay off, I'll add any new information later). Here are those words, in the

form of six banners hung beside each other (no idea how
to format that here, so please go ahead and Google all of
this stuff), all upper case text, each six-line block in
different but uniform colours:

WITH
MEMORY
OF ALL IT
WOULD
LEAVE
UNDONE

FIRST
THROUGH
FOLLY
AND THEN
NOW BY
ERROR

LIKE A
HOPE
AGAINST
HOPE AND
WHATEVER
ELSE

IT WAS
NOW
THERE
AGAIN TO
BE MADE
REAL

HAVING
BEEN
WRITTEN

AT SOME
PRIOR
POINT

IN THE
FACE OF
ALL IT
COULD
HAVE
BECOME

Enigmatic and elusive words, somehow sorrowful,
regretful. Certainly beautiful. Which could lead to a
whole other blog post on how important language is as
something beyond mere communication and more like
art, but I'll resist for now.

Funnier still, this strange journey through some kind of
secret poetic life of my adopted city didn't end there.
Retiring to one of my old favourite haunts in the oldest
part of Vancouver, a little bar in Gastown named the
Irish Heather, all four bathroom doors were festooned
with.... you guessed it.... words. Words written by
Samuel Beckett, Shane MacGowan, Sinéad O'Connor
and Brendan Behan, the latter of which seemed to
encapsulate the day.

"I have a total irreverence
for anything connected
with society,
except that which makes
the roads safer,
the beer stronger,
the food cheaper and
the old men and old women
warmer in the winter and

happier in the summer."

Anyone else know of similar examples in their own cities, where solitary words must compete quietly against the rush of traffic, the roar of floatplanes in the harbour, the blustery cacophony of pigeon wings... and sometimes even triumph?

(For the full visual effect of this article, I strongly suggest you visit it at my blog, The Migrant Type.)

Chapter Seven: The Horror... The Horror...

"Horror... Horror has a face... and you must make a friend of horror." Colonel Kurtz, *Apocalypse Now*

You'd think that horror would be one of the easiest of genres within which to write: create a protagonist who is either extremely likeable or go for the opposite, a character deserving of some particularly overdue and nasty payback; either invent or import a monster from Familiar Horror Trope Land (sparkly or not, preferably the latter); bring them together in some unexpected location and everything gets all squishy and liquidized and unpleasant and the audience members lose all control of their bodily functions and curse your parents... except, that's not necessarily what happens at all. Horror is hard to write. Okay, no, I just lied. Horror is easy to write, but good horror is hard to write.

Turns out you end up with a lot more decisions than you thought: do you go with quiet or splatter, traditional or transgressive, supernatural or psychological, gritty realism or more fanciful and fantastic? And that's only the start. There are questions about suspense, how to build it, sustain it, let it go for a while, bring it back shrieking with ropes of blood-flecked drool and sheer malevolence (that's another thing: beware overwriting; horror as a genre is particularly susceptible). Or endings. Tragic endings are more acceptable in horror than in most fiction, obviously, but does your story earn the especially awful nihilism it culminates in? I mean, what on earth did Frank Darabont think he was doing when he gave his adaptation of Stephen King's "The Mist" *that* ending? You can't give what is after all a solid pulp B-monster-movie, played for some comic moments, the existential, Kafkaesque, sheer dismal bleakness of *that* ending. I mean, come on… sorry, got sidetracked there. Ha. And anyway, film is a whole 'nother area outside of our jurisdiction, thankfully. Point being, this shit gets *complicated*.

It wasn't supposed to be like this. When you picked up your metaphorical Sharpie to write, you were thinking along the lines of something garish, with simple, bold strokes, like a Saturday morning cartoon with scares, a largely fun carnival ride of the mind. It's like you thought to yourself, I'll just go watch Wile E Coyote and Roadrunner—how taxing can that be?—but you somehow forgot about the acid you dropped earlier and now the plight of this desolate, skinny canine with the gaunt, desperate face is making you dig your fingers disconcertingly deep into your *own* face and weep uncontrollably even before he pulls back the ominously creaking arm on that ACME catapult. And then… Every. Single. Horrible. Creak. Sounds. Like. The. Irrevocable. Closing. Of. A. Heavy. Crypt. Door…

But enough of William Shatner's bizarre vocal mannerisms. The point I'm trying to make is that each choice reveals another level or layer, and so on, until you wish you'd never started this horror writing lark and decided to tackle something more simple… like calculus… rendered in Farsi… suspended on an inverted treadmill… over a nest of squirming pit vipers… while balancing a copy of *The Collected Works of H. P. Lovecraft* on your elbow… while solving a minor border dispute between two irritable Central American states.

So as the great—albeit insane—Colonel Kurtz said, you must make a friend of horror. You must learn its mannerisms, its idiosyncrasies, its rhythms and patterns, winks and nods. Its, ha, heart of darkness (God, I annoy myself sometimes). Do not assume you know what makes it tick until you have read a significant number of the greats: H. P. Lovecraft, Bram Stoker, Mary Shelley, Edgar Allan Poe, Robert Bloch, Ray Bradbury, Helen Fielding, Richard Matheson, Ramsey Campbell, John Farris, Peter Straub, Stephen King, Chelsea Quinn Yarbro, Clive Barker, Poppy Z. Brite, Joe R. Lansdale, etc. (One of these things is not like the others.) All joking aside, you need to respect the genre in order to have a chance of writing horror well. Which is not a given. It's no accident the horror genre has been referred to more than once as the redheaded stepchild of genre fiction. But, unless you're out-and-out spoofing it, you need to. That's basically step one.

And this is a mere taster of what you can expect if you're damn fool enough to try your hand at writing horror fiction. In a later chapter, I'll explore further steps that will lead you to some unexpected places, both in the outside world and in your own increasingly demented head. But let me end here with one particularly notable banana skin. One word: bathos. If you don't know it, look it up and we'll wait for you… *hums the theme music from *Top Gun* for some odd and essentially random reason* Done? Okay. Bathos will kill your story, and you will never live down a tale that builds incredible, heart-pounding tension, no matter how deftly or skillfully written, only for the characters to be confronted near the end by—say—a were-hedgehog or a vampire koala. There are some things that will never, ever be frightening. While there may be artistry and prowess in teasing out something disquieting about a bird bath or an old blackboard eraser, for example, you will never squeeze a drop of fear out of a garlic press or a beer coaster. Not even if you make them sparkly.

Chapter Eight: The Book Was Better

"I just saw the movie, wasn't a patch on the book."

If I'd stuffed my face with a deep-fried Mars bar every time I heard this sentiment, I'd probably lose a weigh-in with an elephant seal, have a mouthful of teeth with the average consistency of a sea sponge, and skin the overall texture of pepperoni by now. I'll bet every last one of us has said something similar, though. Which makes every last one of us a bit weird, really. Not quite stupid, but getting there, you know?

Let me explain my thinking. (I find I have to do that a lot, which says nothing good about me whatsoever.)

It's actually quite simple. A book is a book. A movie is a movie. And Popeye is what he is... an extremely odd-shaped sailor with a fetish for canned green vegetables.

Seriously, though, "the book was better" has become one of those irksome knee-jerk phrases that are stand-ins for something else entirely. See: "it's political correctness gone mad!" which actually means "damn, the world doesn't condone my bigotry any more, so I'll just have this here tantrum instead". Or: "I knew them before they were famous" which translates as "I am an unctuous hipster and will drip oily, corrosive scorn on, you know, like, everyone not in the hallowed inner circle of *me*, dude."

But what do we really mean when we utter this phrase? In a mundane sense, I suppose we mean "this apple is better than this orange", but if we already prefer apples to oranges, it doesn't really bear repeating, does it? We could just make that clear once and be done with it: "I am an apple/book person. Not an orange/film person". End of story. No, I think what is happening is similar to when people say "oh, TV, I don't bother watching that stuff any more"—a whole slew of assumptions lie barely hidden beneath the surface, not least of which is that certain media are adjudged inferior. My point isn't to argue whether or not they are, but to lament the smugness of the assumption itself, as if our audience will automatically nod vigorously in agreement every single time.

The complicating factor, I suppose, and one that exposes my metaphor for the flawed and incomplete thing it really is, is that this orange is *based* on that apple in some elusive way. Which shouldn't matter—*it's still a freaking orange!*—yet somehow, to most of us, it does. Why? Are we incorporating a little of the knew-them-before-they-were-famous hipster vibe alongside an assumption that books are inherently superior to movies? Is it because, even after just over a century, movies are still the upstarts? Are we making that hallowed mistake every generation makes, by deploring the newest and latest medium (whether it be jazz, rock'n'roll, comic books, hip-hop or video games, whatever "the kids" are into) in favour of what we are comfortable with? Whatever it is, I wish we'd stop it. It's starting to sound like the jerking of ancient knees, a particularly alarming mix of rubbery creak and twangy groan that makes my stomach feel weird. So yeah, stop it. Please?

Okay, look. There are many novels that have been adapted for film for which any qualitative choice is difficult if not impossible. Let me say it again: a movie is not a book and a book is not a movie. One is pretty much entirely text-based and requires the audience to use imagination and comprehension, whereas the other is almost entirely visual and auditory and requires a little of the same two qualities plus something more elusive. One takes eight or nine hours to ingest, while the other takes around two hours. One is largely a solo project, the other a massive team effort. They are both extremely complex in different ways. Sure, they are related, in that they contain narrative arcs and characters and themes and such things, but they are still very different. Just as a movie and a video game are different. Yes, there are convergences, but overall it makes little sense to judge them by the same metrics.

Anyway, because my OCD side loves lists, I am now going to fire off a random group of 30 books, in no particular order, which weren't better than their movie counterparts, but were simply different. Not better, not worse, different. Like apples. Like oranges. Like Popeye. Like deep-fried Mars bars. Okay, those last things are bad.

1. *Charlie and the Chocolate Factory* by Roald Dahl (renamed *Willy Wonka and the Chocolate Factory* in the original movie adaptation).
2. *The Body* by Stephen King (renamed *Stand By Me* in Rob Reiner's film version)
3. *The Shining* by Stephen King
4. *2001: A Space Odyssey* by Arthur C. Clarke
5. *Do Androids Dream of Electric Sheep?* by Philip K. Dick (renamed *Blade Runner* in Ridley Scott's classic film)
6. *Trainspotting* by Irvine Welsh
7. *The Big Sleep* by Raymond Chandler
8. *Psycho* by Robert Bloch
9. *Atonement* by Ian McEwan

10. *The Lord of the Rings* by J. R. R. Tolkien (combine Peter Jackson's trilogy for the comparison)
11. *Mystic River* by Dennis Lehane
12. *To Kill a Mockingbird* by Harper Lee
13. *A Clockwork Orange* by Anthony Burgess
14. *One Flew Over The Cuckoo's Nest* by Ken Kesey
15. *On the Beach* by Nevil Shute
16. *Deliverance* by James Dickey
17. *The Grapes of Wrath* by John Steinbeck
18. *The Silence of the Lambs* by Thomas Harris
19. *Children of Men* by P. D. James
20. *Misery* by Stephen King
21. *No Country For Old Men* by Cormac McCarthy
22. *Wuthering Heights* by Emily Brontë (the best film being the 1939 version)
23. *The World According to Garp* by John Irving
24. *The Godfather* by Mario Puzo
25. *The Dead* by James Joyce
26. *Fight Club* by Chuck Palahniuk
27. *The Hours* by Michael Cunningham
28. *Wonder Boys* by Michael Chabon
29. *American Psycho* by Bret Easton Ellis
30. *The Name of the Rose* by Umberto Eco

Note the mix of classic lit, contemporary lit and genre fiction… No real reason, just note it… Okay, I admit it, I was going to make a great point there and completely forgot what it was. Cough. Moving on… Wait! I was just gonna note that I'm by no means stacking loaded thumbs on the dice by picking weaksauce novels/stories here. They're all at least good and many of them are great. And yet, aside from the occasional glaring piece of wrongness, such as *The Bonfire of the Vanities* or *Moby-Dick*, not one of these film versions is significantly inferior, or even inferior at all, some being arguably superior. Certainly my point stands that you can make a case for either incarnation. An argument can also be made, based on a closer study of these successes, perhaps, that a film—recognizing itself as a different animal entirely—may often work better if it doesn't try too hard to replicate the source material.

Anyway, dear reader, since I've only included works with which I'm familiar in both mediums, you will no doubt come up with your own equally impressive list with which to bolster or shred my theory. Let me know, I'm not hard to find.

Chapter Nine: Entitled

Oh my god, okay, so there's this thing, right? Did you hear? There are these people, just ordinary people like you and me except they got lucky because there's this revolution going on and people are bulldozing the libraries all across America *right now* and taking apart those Barns'n'No-Bull stores or whatever they're called, which is, ha, funny, because it's like that saying about locking the barn door after... anyway, I gotta tell you this, it's so cool, and you'll never believe it, but back to these lucky folks, one of them is called Joe Konehead and there's even this really young chick named Amanda Hawking (I think she's the little sister of that handicapped spacegeek with the creepy computer voice), and they heard about this new book revolution, only they're not books, they're *eBooks* and, oh my god, LOL, this is so amazing, you gotta keep listening. So they made, like, more money than Jesus at a Casino thanks to these iKindles and MaxiPads and all the other eReaders that all these big companies are now making especially for the eBooks, and you know, here's the thing, you can now go sell your eBooks on them since it's so easy, anyone can do it...

What's that? No, you don't have to be like Walt Shakespeare or even that Dan Vinci & Co dude, you know? Seriously. You don't need to worry about the writing. It's not like your high school English class any more, with all those Mice and Mockingbirds and a bunch of hillbillies with weird names like Spartacus Lynch who sound like totally uncool racists, lol—you know, those classes everyone knew were stupid and wouldn't help you in life in any way *what-so-ever*. No, it's all done for you in the software, now, and you get it all formatted for you when you upchuck it to Amazon or whatever, or this other website called Crushwords that literally crushes up all your words and spits them out of an actual meat grinder along with a really helpful manual that you honestly don't really need to read, and it's so cool... only you don't actually see it, it's all done behind the scenes... although I don't exactly know how they separate the bits of shredded paper from the ground beef afterward... but moving on...!

What's that? Editing? Nah, Squishwords and Amazon do all that for you, you don't need to bother with it because you'll be busy rounding up new words to join together for your next book because it's all about *mo-men-tum* and you also have to market it, so what you do is you get someone to help you set up a blog on WordLess.org or Booger.com or whatever and you don't need to do much, just put in one of those blue lines you click on which takes you to where your eBook is selling like hot, juicy, word-drenched cakes as you watch the money pouring into your PlayPen account while you sign books and look awesome and adorable having your photo taken and shit.

By the way, you guys, I like the word eBooks because the "e" part sounds like the noise inside my head, you know? Eeeeeeeeeeee. ROFL! LOL!

Oh, and here's a big secret I'm gonna tell you, because I'm going to wet my Lululemons if I don't: all you gotta do is write about vampires. Or dragons. And guess what? You shouldn't make them too scary because you have to write for most people, who are all pretty much major wusses, but here's the really neat part... ha, ha...

you make them fall in love. Just like it would happen in real life.

Huh? Story? No, you don't need to worry, every book ever written has basically one story line. Boy meets girl. Boy loses girl. Boy gets girl again. Or here, if you want to be really clever, just reverse the sexes, lol! See? I'm brilliant! Anyway, just follow that formula and give your characters super-awesome names... oh, and find a really bright, sappy cover, don't forget, because you need to be noticed in the marketplace, because since those first lucky folks struck gold, a whole boatload of others have joined the bandwagon... isn't that typical?... and because of that, we have to stand out from the crowd by yelling "buy my book!" louder and louder, and by going to all our friends on Facebook and Twitter and telling them to download our stuff or they're not even our friends really they're just jealous... LOL!... and don't forget to drop into as many groups as you can and tell *complete strangers* on the internet they better buy your book because it's the only way anyone will notice it otherwise. No, no, they won't get upset, it's called *Cap-it-al-ism* and it's what makes us all American. Everyone's doing it.

Because, see, we're undies, got it? That stands for undependent because we're not dependent on the old record companies any more, that's what I read on *Mushable* once, that Numbster changed the whole ballgame and now these Random Penguins and Simon Shyster types are wondering what happened while the undie revolution literally killed off all the literary agents and editors after torturing them with horrible mangled grammar and buried them in a warehouse in Brooklyn I think where all the mob bosses go to mourn the death of the Big Six, which is what they call all the old Sicilian families now they've lost the publishing wars. Or, I might have got that slightly wrong, but you get the gist, yeah?

It's a whole new world and we can make our fame and fortune on the internet, better even than Snooks and The Situation because this is *post*-TV, baby, this is the newest, sparkliest thing.

Ha, all those people ever since high school calling me a bubblehead or a dialtone, you watch me get the last laugh, me an author and everything. 'Cos yeah, I'm not even a writer, I'm gonna be an *author*, which means I am like the next level of writer, like when you go up a level in that War of the Worldscraft game my little brother plays, ROFL. Hey, wasn't Tom Cruise in that movie? Anyway, you can eat my dust, Tom *loser* Cruise because I am going to set up my tent right there on the red carpet and the paparazzi will be begging me for upskirts of my sparkly vajayjay but I'm no headshaving, stubbleslitted wackjob like Brit became and they won't ever get them, just the *promise* of them, because the secret is to milk it, and this chick's fame is gonna last a lot longer than some stupid 15 minutes like that Limey tennis player Andy Warthog used to say. I mean, *think* about it. Writers… sorry, *authors*…stay famous *way* longer than movie stars, even. Shakespeare, who I already mentioned, has been well known now for well over a hundred years, going back even before *DiCaprio* was born! Think about that! Ohmygod, ohmygod, so excited! *Claps enthusiastically*

Chapter Ten: The Power at Our Fingertips

In this chapter, I want to demonstrate the power of what Mark Coker (Smashwords) calls the "rise of the indie author collective" (*The Secrets to Ebook Publishing Success*). Indies Unlimited is every bit a part of that rise, that *revolution* really, one that has eroded the power of traditional publishing and significantly democratized the entire process.

Now, there are as many tips and tricks out there for helping independent authors "maximize their brand" or "utilize the tools of the internet" as there are slightly dodgy-looking punters at a female mud wrestling contest, and the debate continues to rage over the effectiveness of reciprocal Facebook "liking" or Amazon "tagging" every bit as fiercely as it does over that of Mona's standing moonsault and tilt-a-whirl crossbody press on Dolores back in Round Five.

And I have no more answers to those questions than your average... well, dodgy-looking punter at a female mud... But enough of that; in the tradition of great pitchmen everywhere... I wanna tell ya about what works, folks!

On March 17, the redoubtable Jim Devitt (Indies Unlimited), showed us a neat if at-first-glance confusing trick. Well, confusing if, like me, you're more than a little dense when it comes to the arcane ways of the mighty Amazon dot com. In his post, Jim explained a method by which you change what is known as the "category path" of your book on its Amazon page and effectively reduce its number of competitors by fine-tuning that path, or string. Now, I'm not going to completely humiliate myself by outlining each and every wrong turn I took after my initial wild misinterpretations of Jim's instructions. Suffice it to say that, after a number of emails between Amazon and my heartbreakingly clueless self, I did manage to end up with two slightly more customized category paths. Read Jim's post—including the comments section in which I also humiliate myself publicly (okay, sensing a theme here)—for a much better nuts-and-bolts explanation than I could honestly provide (I can do nuts, no problem, just not bolts).

But the point is that I did finally arrive at these two new paths, and noticed that in one of them in particular (Kindle Store > Kindle eBooks > Nonfiction > Travel > United States > States > New York > New York City), I was already ranked at #4. It so happened that someone bought my book that day and I noticed it move up to #2. Which is when it dawned on me that if I asked enough people to buy it over one short, frenzied period of time, there was a chance it could make the #1 slot, however temporarily, thus giving me a *bona fide* Amazon #1 Bestseller! The only question: how far ahead in Amazon's mysterious ranking algorithms was the current #1 seller in that particular category path, and was it catchable? I didn't know. But I wanted to find out.

So I called in all my favours from the boys downtown… well okay, from my slightly bemused and mainly bespectacled writing cohorts and colleagues from within various Facebook groups. Essentially begging them to buy my book, I even lowered the price, which is the equivalent of leaning into the open passenger side window and flashing acres of cleavage while making kissy faces. Not a good look, in other words. And perhaps my lowest point to date as an independent writer was when I found myself with my finger poised over the **Buy Now With 1-Click** button… and clicked. Yes, I admit it here for the world to mock me with: *I bought my own book.* For which I later did penance by dragging razor wire through my spleen and driving carpet nails into my perineum.

But also, some very kind people, most of them my colleagues and cohorts in the indie writer community, felt sufficient ~~excruciating embarrassment~~ sympathy for my plight that they dug deep and shelled out for my lonely little book. Cue a couple of tense hours with my finger poised like a woodpecker with OCD, sporadically refreshing the Amazon page and watching the ranking (what on earth did we do for fun before the internet? Torture the kids with crocodile clips and car batteries? Prank the neighbours with elaborate setups involving loud hailers, flamethrowers and wolverine feces? Oh wait, yeah, we read books), until… well, it worked. Just like that.

I was gobsmacked. #1 in an admittedly gerrymandered category, but no matter. It was a real bestseller. Which is especially ironic, since it has never sold well, being both short and nonfiction; pretty much guaranteed niche market material. In fact, I don't mind admitting that its usual *overall* ranking fluctuates somewhere between 200,000 and 400,000. And that brings me to another point: the book's overall Amazon Kindle Store ranking peaked at around 22,000, which prompts me to ask: if a small number of near-simultaneous purchases is enough to lift one eBook hundreds of thousands of places in the Amazon lists, are the vast majority of eBooks really selling as well as we've been led to believe? Is this an example of the so-called long tail, and did I just witness my own book advance from its usual place partway down the tail to somewhere nearer the front... yet still essentially a part of the tail? Okay, we're getting into areas outside my expertise, which is admittedly not difficult, but it's nutrition for cogitation, don't you think?

What I take from this, however, is that the power of social media and our potential for collective action gave me a bestseller, as it could give *you* a bestseller, and as much as an observer might accuse us of gaming the system, we still put in the effort and discovered it was possible. And that surely stands for something in a world in which the little guy often feels excluded by the arcane rules of gargantuan corporations; rules that appear only to benefit those already at the top. Hey, Coker's right. We're not so little after all, not when we're many.

Chapter Eleven: The Method, Man

An older post by Dan Mader on Indies Unlimited is pertinent here. In it, he goes all Wu Tang on our collective be-hinds, extolling the benefits of "the crew", of having a cadre of peers with which to bounce ideas off of, collaborate with, borrow from, represent to, and party alongside till you're hoarse and vacant. He has a point. Writers are horribly misanthropic for the most part, and that solitary nature can be toxic when left to its own unhealthy and addictive devices. I call it the writer's paradox: we spend most of our time alone figuring out how to communicate with people. I mean, really. How utterly ludicrous is that?

So, I was trying to come up with ideas for this chapter while in the type of mood Mussolini was probably in around the time those Italian partisans captured him and hung him on a meat hook, only a much lower grade version, obviously, and was about to burn more bridges than all the desperate, self-hating trolls in and around Madison County by writing something pointlessly scattershot-angry to be read by pretty much anyone on any platform anywhere, which you don't need me to say would have been astoundingly, mindbogglingly *dumb*, when I found myself in a conversation with the very same Mader and K.S. "Kat" Brooks (which sounds like a Savile Row tailor shop, or maybe part of a law firm: Mader, Mader and Brooks) and they allowed me to rant for a period while they snuck occasional glances at each other, no doubt wondering how they were going to inform my loved ones, until I eventually ran out of steam and left an awkward, very pregnant silence. Not to mention the mother of all run-on sentences.

After which they suggested with exquisite, admirable patience that I tone down the outrage and frustration slightly, and instead of skewering my formless targets with sharpened words, I sweeten the whole deal with an extended metaphor. For which you, kind reader, will henceforth be the beneficiary. Starting now:

I love music. I adore music. Music has saved my life. Music has preserved my last shreds of sanity. Music has taught me as much as any other human activity, including books. Like many who become obsessed with consuming something, I eventually tried to produce it. I saved my paper route money and picked up a small Spanish guitar for less than £20 when I was around 12, then a horribly battered Strat copy a year or so later for around the same price, for which a friend of mine built a battery powered 10-Watt amp so we could go annoy woodland creatures by playing distorted versions of "Stairway To Heaven" and "Anarchy in the UK" in bucolic settings (squirrels in particular have an aversion to the Sex Pistols, I've discovered).

As we all pretty much did back then (music lessons were for those middle class kids who owned handkerchiefs and didn't drink from jars with chips around their rims), I basically taught myself to play—jamming with friends who were better, playing along to my worn records and cassettes, painstakingly rewinding and playing, rewinding and playing… until I noticed something that troubled me.

A small matter, perhaps, but basically, I sucked.

Don't get me wrong, I learned a bunch of chords over the years, a variety of rhythmic strumming patterns (if three constitutes a "variety") and even some picking techniques (if by "some picking techniques" I mean "two slightly different ways of moving my thumb and forefinger"). I was and remain an enthusiastic guitar player and have spent untold years collecting and transcribing chords and simple guitar tablature for many of my favourite songs, which I have inflicted on mercifully few bystanders given the sheer volume of songs I've managed to amass.

Because it bears repeating: I suck.

My singing voice is reminiscent of the sound you made that time you grated your thumb halfway down to the first knuckle instead of the chunk of fresh Parmesan. Hearing it makes honey badgers think it's mating season. I've set off alarms. Triggered border skirmishes. Oh, and I'm not tone deaf. I can actually sing in key and everything. But then, that's like saying Justin Bieber can wield a paintbrush. It's meaningless on too many levels to even bother unpacking. The fact remains, I have the self-awareness to realize that my career as a musician was basically stillborn from the moment I tried to play *that* riff from "Smoke on the Water" alone in my bedroom. I may be a complete idiot but I'm not stupid.

All of which saved me the headache of a lifetime of figuring out what time signatures are, as well as the heartache of telling my special friend back home that the oozing, alarmingly lurid rash in my bathing suit area was from sitting too long on hot, sweaty tour buses and had nothing to do with those silly groupies you, ha ha, might have, you know, heard about from an irresponsibly sensationalist media, baby.

So. I'm not taking up space on stage, or anywhere. I don't have to yell above the fray to get noticed, to land that elusive recording contract, perhaps hit that stage while modeling burlap rainbow lederhosen and rubber nun suits or setting fire to fruit bat entrails and whipping them around my howling, desperate head while silently urging those A&R dudes from Sony BMG who just have to be scattered throughout the audience, to *notice* me, goddamnit, acknowledge my inherent genius, make me the star I know I should be…

As I said, I'm not doing any of that.

And the world sighs in sweet, blessed relief. Because I knew. All along. I knew I couldn't turn the sow's ear of my musical "talent" into the silk purse of a career. In other words, I had only half the prerequisites, which wasn't enough: a deep and abiding love for music but nowhere near the talent. I even tried writing songs but they were essentially sounds stuck together with modeling glue and yarn. Love, but no talent. At least I had half.

But writing is different. And that's all I'm saying. That's *all* I'm saying. Now go. Figure it out. Scoot. I can feel that pissy mood coming back…

Chapter Twelve: I Love You

Here, in reverse order, are ten things I like that are related to writing. Sort of. This is a completely random list and may possibly be an early sign of my eventual and catastrophic disintegration. Actually, I've just reread it and it makes a very abstract kind of sense, after all. If you're a surrealist. Or a nutbar. Or a strange gelatinous creature from the Aldebaran system.

10. I like hats. Not to wear. Very rarely, in fact, do I wear hats. I am far too proud of my flowing golden locks to hide them. I run my fingers through those locks while mimicking the sound of gentle lovemaking in haylofts. Anyway, hats. I will write about hats until the cows come home. And if, upon arriving home, those same cows eat all the hats, I will create more hats from whole cloth. Only, not. I'll create them from nothing but thoughts, like Lewis Carroll embracing Khalil Gibran while on acid. The flowing golden locks part was a lie, incidentally. It's normal guy hair, short and greying, but I still like it.

9. Roy Batty. The coolest of replicants, steeped in pride and melancholy like a lost boy in a gymnasium full of parakeets. I wish I could have written something even a tenth as poignant and plain badass-cool as the "tears in rain" soliloquy. Actually, this isn't good. This actually makes me want to give up writing. As it should. You should too. And when I do, I will sigh, with the staggering weight of humanity's eternal sorrow behind my exhalation, and whisper "time to die."

8. Poetry. Poetry is very cool, it's just that most of it isn't. But the good stuff, the *good* stuff... Here:

"Maybe, as he stood
two inches from the wall,
in darkness, fogging the old plaster
with his breath, he visualized the future
as a mansion standing on the shore
that he was rowing to
with his tongue's exhausted oar."

from *Self Improvement* by Tony Hoagland

Or:

"On longer evenings,
Light, chill and yellow,
Bathes the serene
Foreheads of houses.
A thrush sings,
Laurel-surrounded
In the deep bare garden,
Its fresh-peeled voice
Astonishing the brickwork.
It will be spring soon,
It will be spring soon –
And I, whose childhood
Is a forgotten boredom,
Feel like a child
Who comes on a scene
Of adult reconciling,
And can understand nothing
But the unusual laughter,
And starts to be happy."

Coming by Philip Larkin

49

Poetry is not being all emo about how no one understands you, especially that girl with the cute dimples and the endearing way she flicks her hair back. When it comes to poetry, most of us get stuck in that phase and forget to move into the adult world, thinking such ephemera poetry. It's understandable in a way. We are not always taught it with joy. But poetry is neither Hallmark doggerel nor a sterile academic sideshow. At its best, it's more akin to music, with its odd internal logic, tone and rhythmic/melodic qualities. Each type of poem has its own rules. A sonnet is not even close to a poem written in free verse, but both are equally valid as forms, the skill of the poet and the (mind's) ear of the audience the only things that matter. The good stuff isn't easy to find; you have to dig. I could post maybe a hundred examples right now of why good poetry is worth your time. It's inspiring. It's the use of delicacy and subtlety within exacting strictures. It's beauty. I don't know why, but for many centuries poets were valued, yet if you say you're a poet today (I don't, because I'm not), you will likely be met with awkward silence or possibly even the mocking laughter of a growing crowd that quickly senses blood. In the shame scales, it's perhaps only a rung above sex offender, or even politician. I'm really not sure why. But I like it. Good poetry, that is. Is there a person alive who wouldn't react in some way to such a startling phrase as "astonishing the brickwork"?

7. Why don't North Americans "get" what they insist on calling soccer? It's inspirational. The very criticisms they level at it are the aspects that make it more than a sport, something elevated into a hybrid of art form and planetary-wide cult. Take the low scoring. It really should be obvious to anyone who has thought about gold or diamonds or raw lovemaking on a killing field why that is a positive. When you make the goals so rare, their value is increased. They are precious. I watch soccer, or football as I used to call it back when I was European, and something of its grace and power and drama has to inform my writing. At least, I hope it does. It has to. Even the simulation must translate. I dive to win a penalty. Metaphorically. Even when you dive, you still have to tuck it away. The crowd is outraged. It's wrong, yet you now have a chance to win. I can't explain this. It has something to do with the inherent unfairness of the universe. Randomness and a terrible unquenched need.

6. I love you. And I will make you love me back.

5. I am not judgmental. Not generally. But if I encounter someone who doesn't like animals I am creeped the fuck out. I have created characters still only at the sketch stage who are lacking in empathy and capable of great brutality, and I instinctively make them animal-haters. This I might never change.

4. Do you recall an early morning in which the air is cool yet already embracing the promise of the sun? In which the simple act of breathing is a delight albeit one containing the chill woe of its eventual absence? In which the shadows are still soft yet beginning to test their edges like a hoodlum with a switchblade grinning in an alley? I don't know what I'm trying to say, but this dark, dichotomous urgency is filling me with the strangest panic.

3. It's all about writing. Which is essentially communication. Which, in its turn, is how we connect with our fellow humans. So, it's about love. Because we can't love any *one* or any *thing* if we surrender to the awful void of the world's loneliness. Isolation is narcissism. When we magically talk to another, and we get even a portion of our meaning across, with all its beauty or frustration or uncertainty or hunger, we are performing the work we once attributed to gods. It's alchemical. It's akin to magic. Love can't fully happen without it. I take back what I said earlier: we should never give up writing. It would be like a bird giving up the air.

2. I don't know what this chapter is about. It isn't funny, or even profound. We sometimes have strange days in which the quirky detritus of the world comes drifting in on rays of alien light via windows we didn't know existed. Once we know they exist, it's important not to board them up, yet equally important we don't force their eldritch light to shine. Let them shine when they shine, and otherwise remain shrouded.

1. A woman stood on a promontory. She clasped a dead kitten to her breasts, and the look of sorrow on her face made the gods weep so much they lost their nerve and abandoned humanity. She looked down at the wrathful surf below, at its inexplicable tantrum against the snaggletoothed rocks and she knew both the ocean's rage and it's deceptive placidity. She swayed. A sudden gust would plunge her toward those rocks. She held her breath and waited to see if nature would further aid and abet a terrible crime against love, a crime of neglect. She leaned forward at an almost impossible angle. But no gust, not even a breeze. Nature was violent below, yet gentle as lark song up here on the cliff edge. The sun's rays were splayed above the horizon, gilt-edging the few clouds amid the deepening blue of the sky. She let her tears fall and recalled a time when she had been a little girl and thought she had seen a stunted demon steal across the school playing fields, hunched and hooded and malignant as any inoperable cancer, as hostile a thing as any she had encountered before or since. She cried for the kitten that had been denied its chance to accept or reject the glory and the disenchantment, the splendour and the defilement. She held its tiny grey body out, marveling at its lightness, and she let it fall to the tumultuous indifference of the eternal clash of water and rock below. The way of yielding and the way of resistance. Thinking about the many ways we must choose to either love or murder, she turned toward home and the man who might soon pay the price—deserved or otherwise—of her eventual decision.

Chapter Thirteen: I Have No Idea

So you got this deadline for your latest blog post/chapter/writing assignment and all you can hear in your head is a sound resembling the distant whine of an overclocked laptop crossed with Mariah Carey conducting elaborate experiments involving helium and canary embryos. Essentially, a combination of blind panic and a sheer lack of anything resembling an idea. You briefly consider opening your carotid artery while gargling with paint thinner before saying to yourself "way too dramatic", so you dial it down and rock back and forth making mewling noises instead.

But the ticking clock is relentless, and something has to give. This is your last chance to become a mother… oh, wait, different story altogether. Sorry. Got my notes mixed up… So, anyway, what do you do? Well, you consult my newly patented **Top Ten List of Idea Generators and Writing Exercises**, is what! In the spirit of heroic cartoon supermice everywhere, here they come to save the day…

1. You are an international jewel thief. You have just fenced enough ice to re-sink the Titanic. You are flush. You receive a phone call in which a heavily disguised voice says, "I am stranded in the Philippines. I am not Stephen Hise, never even heard of him in fact, but just so you know, the awesome website Indies Unlimited could sure use some serious funding right about now." What do you do?

2. Push an elderly lady into traffic and describe the aftermath. An alternate version would be to record the sound of an audio-assisted crosswalk, find a home for the visually impaired next to a busy street and wait for the residents to emerge, at which point you press Play on your recording device. Remember to describe the ensuing events in loving detail. It's the hilarious aftermath we're looking for in particular.

3. Ponder this simple question and then write down your thoughts: why is the word "phonetically" not spelled phonetically? And, for a bonus: why does "succinct" have two syllables? Do you think words can commit fraud? Did Emily Brontë completely make up the word "wuthering"? And, anyway, how badass is it that she has umlauts in her name?

4. Eat something you hate, such as boiled wombat elbows or rancid yak butter. Make sure the very thought of it already induces a degree of nausea. Follow it up with a plate of traditional English cuisine. Yes, that is redundant, I know. Drink a bottle of cod liver oil. Follow that up with a few shot glasses of hot sauce. Nurture some genuine anger in the pit of your stomach. (If you find you are unable to do this, turn on FOX News.) Locate a trampoline. Bounce on it repeatedly. If you possess sufficient athleticism, perform a few backflips. If not, keep bouncing. Dismount. Find a giant canvas and stand over it. Or squat, your call. Let nature take its course, in whatever way it chooses. Then, in 500 words, describe the resulting art work.

5. Write a Petrarchan Sonnet that includes the following elements: a banjo, a dispirited clown, two befuddled paranormal investigators, a lighthouse keeper with bipolar disorder and a lukewarm vat of seahorse droppings. Please remember: use iambic pentameter and an octave of

$$\text{a b b a a b b a}$$

and a more flexible sestet of

$$\text{c d c d c d}$$

or

$$\text{c d d c d c}$$

6. Free-write longhand for ten minutes. No cue, no topic. Just write. Do not take your pen off the paper. Go!

7. Write a series of short literary mashups. Why should musicians have all the fun, after all? For example, mimic the writing style of Ernest Hemingway while employing the subject matter of H. P. Lovecraft. You may call the final product *The Old Man And Cthulhu*, for instance. Or combine the style of Cormac McCarthy, perhaps, with a Dr. Seuss theme: "The sun did not shine. The Cat in the Hat raised his face to the god-abandoned day. Thing One was uncoupled from its shoring, everything grey in the world's last dawn. Oh Fish in the Pot, he whispered. Oh Fish." You get the idea.

8. If you write horror, try a chick lit story. If your preferred genre is paranormal romance, write a western. The world needs more Gucci zombies and levitating cowboys, after all.

9. Write a long piece outlining your thoughts on why JFK's assassination might have been connected to an obscure standard bearer in the Duke of Wellington's army at Waterloo. Be sure to include the rare yet incisive commentary by one Dwight Z. Finkelheimer, who famously postulated that the bell jar in Sylvia Plath's famous novel was actually a metaphor for hair metal band Motley Crüe's insistence on delivering tanning beds to orphanages, all of which culminates eerily in architect Frank Gehry's blueprint for cloning Lee Harvey Oswald, providing him with a blowgun filled with toxic paperclips and setting him loose amid a throng of Jesuit priests riding gloriously oblivious and slightly dim alpacas, the prized wool of which will one day clothe the very standard bearer mentioned previously. Woah. I don't know about you, but *I* got goosebumps.

10. Notice that writing is not an art or a science; it's an exercise in sheer futility. It is a slow, quiet, lonely torment; less a long, dark night of the soul and more a longer, grey afternoon of the spleen. It is reminiscent of the feeling you might get if a beaming child-faced serial killer peeled off your skin a layer at a time while reciting the complete works of obscure Scottish poet William McGonagall and sprinkling apple cider vinegar on your exposed, suppurating flesh. Reminiscent, albeit not exact. It is possibly the world's most stupid human activity, and considering those activities include Australian dwarf tossing and British shin-kicking contests as well as Japanese game shows featuring a Snooki lookalike and a man disguised as Rasputin performing disquieting rituals inside giant hamster balls, that's got to be pretty stupid. It all just makes you want to cry for your momma, not only now, but every single moment that remains of your miserable life. Now, once you have absorbed this, go away and write a counter argument, providing rich examples of why I am wrong, while being careful to note the fact that none of this will matter to you in less than a hundred years, since you will be dead. Which may be ugly, but it's the truth. As ugly a truth as the one about Mother Teresa and the one-legged insurance salesman in that Calcutta alleyway. But don't write about that. Write instead of how the mind goes, of its inevitable ruin. Oh look, a flower. Florentine death squads. The Mitt Romney remix. Castigation. Fuel. Aphids.

Chapter Fourteen: Catharsis or Carnival?

As anyone connected to the horror genre can tell you, we get more than our fair share of questions that boil down to "why do you read/write that stuff?" along with the accompanying nervous sidelong looks and wrinkled nose gestures. And, put on the spot, I've always found it difficult to give a reasoned answer, settling for either the glib ("because I'm more twisted than a yoga mom wrestling with a Slinky in a pretzel machine") or the cop-out (a bewildered shrug). So when Sue Palmer from Book Junkies did me the recent kindness of asking me a far more nuanced and generously-phrased version of that question, I snapped her hand off and wrote down some thoughts. Only, I didn't actually snap her hand off. That's a metaphor, thankfully. Here are those thoughts, and I think they come closest to capturing what it is about the genre that attracts me, repels me, keeps me coming back as a reader, writer and even viewer. Well, all this and the euphoric thrill of the carnival ride, too; let's not forget that.

Horror is the only genre named after an emotion, and a very specific feeling at that. Which is strange when you think about it. I mean, why don't we call comedy "hilarity", or drama "alarm"? But this one word doesn't really do it justice, since we can experience everything from terror to revulsion to disquiet when reading a horror story. I think this provides a lot more scope than is immediately obvious, and the genre has always suffered from a perception of distaste. Or plain bad taste. Something it has fully and even gleefully embraced on occasion. I think it's far more rich and varied than the casual reader often assumes, however, and its effects can range from the thrill ride at the carnival to sheer gross-out to a sense of true and deep unease. Escapism? Catharsis? The arguments have raged on that one for centuries.

I wish I could cite just one author as my main inspiration, but I'd have to reel off a list. I suppose Stephen King comes closest, in terms of his dazzling and prolific storytelling ability, although my own stories tend not to lean toward the supernatural as much as King's do. Clive Barker, for his sheer writing chops, his unrelenting willingness to go places most shy away from and his complex imaginative world-building, would be another.

My own tastes tend toward the darkly psychological and even surreal. If you could somehow meld Barker's technical wizardry with King's storytelling and throw in some David Lynch, you might get what I am trying to achieve when I write horror. I suppose the best word to sum that up would be dread. A kind of bleak yet strangely or fleetingly beautiful unease. The agony of that elusive beauty amid the sewer. I am intrigued by exactly how far down into the earth that old disused well really goes. And not so much what lives in it but what lives within *us* when we find ourselves down there.

As for modern horror, I think it is currently as diverse as it has ever been. With everything from the *Twilight* series (not a fan, but each to his or her own) to both *American Horror Story* and *The Walking Dead* on television, there seems to be a resurgence in those traditional horror tropes I tend not to be as interested in (zombies are my one exception to this, as they seem almost plausible in a world in which genetic experimentation, environmental disaster and deadly viruses are not only possible but actual realities). And recent horror film is a rich smorgasbord, with incredible 21st Century pickings such as *Audition, Let the Right One in, Martyrs, Oldboy, Antichrist, Rec*, and hundreds of others I could reel off here (ha, I said "reel"). But I don't complain about even the more lightweight stuff, as I remember times when the horror genre was brushed under the carpet, treated like the red-headed stepchild of all genre writing, basically looked down upon. For this renaissance, King must take a huge amount of credit. That said, I don't think a genre that explores some of the darker sides of our nature will ever be accepted by the mainstream, for good or for ill. There will be plenty who see it as exploitative or sensational or even childish, and oddly, some of those same people will laud Shakespeare, Oscar Wilde, the Grimm brothers, Charles Dickens, Henry James, Daphne du Maurier, etc., all of whom wrote horror at some point.

There are so many branches, however: the religion-based terror of *The Exorcist* is a world away from the transgressive horror of, say, Dennis Cooper or Poppy Z. Brite. The late-'80s horror resurgence that gave birth to the so-called splatterpunks (Skipp, Spector, Lansdale) was also the era in which Peter Straub's literary and darkly imaginative work was ascendant. Or Ramsey Campbell's near-hallucinogenic nightmare visions of urban decay. John Farris, too (now there's a relatively unheralded master). And yet they are equally capable of shocking. Or disturbing. Again, why some readers should want to be disturbed escapes me, but in a world where babies are sometimes raped and bayoneted in front of their parents, or in which our bodies can turn on themselves and literally eat us alive, I don't blame horror writers for reflecting that and trying to wrestle with how truly awful things can get, how deeply, sickeningly violent humans can become. Writers write about the human condition, after all. Perhaps if I can tell some of these stories while shedding some light on the terrible darkness, there's a glimmer of healing. Or maybe I and my fellow horror fans/writers are kidding ourselves and all we really want is that thrill ride on the roller coaster. Or maybe it's some of each. I honestly don't know. But thanks to my work with abused kids, I do know this: telling stories can be how we deal with trauma; in fact, relating our "truths" out loud is essential to what trauma experts have called "critical incident stress debriefing" and perhaps that, in the end, is the root impulse of the genre we've chosen to term "horror"—that by telling each other how it felt to meet the boogeyman, we're simply trying to heal.

Chapter Fifteen: The Good, The Bad, The Indifferent

I've discovered a potentially fatal flaw in my personality. I mean, outside the more obvious ones (pointing them out would be redundant if you've read this far already). Put simply, I like genre and I like literary. In musical terms, I like teen pop and modern classical, Spears and Stockhausen, Avril and Arvo. But this chapter is neither a demonstration of my "amazing" pop cultural eclecticism nor a reflection of my mental health anxieties; we like what we like, after all. No, this section is an attempt to reconcile two apparently opposing impulses in the world of writing: the aforementioned (alleged) impasse between genre and literary fiction.

For anyone who has attended a university-level creative writing course, even a single workshop, this dichotomy might already have raised its slightly distorted head. I majored in English literature at the University of Manchester, England, and I've also attended a one-year certificate course in creative writing at a local university (Simon Fraser University's The Writer's Studio), and I don't regret either of them. My purpose here is certainly not to trash the rarefied air of academia. Far from it. Because I genuinely learned a great deal about writing— about what works and what doesn't work, about the inner alchemy and the outer pragmatism of this eccentric world—from those two experiences. Not to mention the confidence boost of sharing your work among motivated and engaged peers as deeply in love with the written word as you, alongside the equally essential practice of reading in front of an audience so you don't forget that word's spoken nature either.

But. There's a prevailing wisdom within such circles that genre is inferior to literary fiction. It's either implied or stated overtly. That one is entertainment and one is art. One is frivolous and disposable, the other profound and eternal. (Interestingly, we hear the same, equally dicey "received wisdoms" in music criticism. A *received* wisdom is usually an unexamined one, after all.)

I've thought about this long and hard. Which isn't especially easy for me. So bear with me. I write in many forms. I've written music reviews, poetry, many styles of fiction, nonfiction, journalism, articles and essays. Although I've been told my own writing style is "literary", and believe there is plenty to admire in that category, I don't ever intentionally set out to write "literary" fiction. I love the writing of Ian McEwan, which is considered predominantly literary by those who define such things, but I also read Stephen King's predominantly genre material every bit as avidly.

I sometimes wonder whether we're overly restricting ourselves.

Let's, for the sake of argument, deny that a firm delineation between the two even exists. Why would one contain more "art" than the other, after all? Fiction itself is a genre, alongside its siblings and cousins poetry, lyric prose, creative nonfiction, journalism, etc. Likewise, writing itself is a kind of genre, alongside music, dance, theatre, film and the visual arts in general.

See where I'm going with this? I hope so, because I don't.

But seriously, why would we arbitrarily assign less significance to any one particular level or manifestation of "genre"? We don't tend to ascribe a deeper resonance to writing over, say, dance. Or sculpture over theatre. Nor do we elevate detective fiction above, say, science fiction, other than for admittedly subjective reasons of personal taste. Then why this line drawn between "literary" and "genre"? What does it mean, and what does it say a) about us, and b) about the works we assign to each category.

My experience has been that between the extreme caricatures of navel-fixated ivory towers on the one hand and outright penny-dreadful hackery on the other, most fiction writers fall into some great amorphous blob somewhere in the middle. Who is to say whether Cormac McCarthy's *Blood Meridian* is genre (horror, western, adventure, western horror adventure) fiction or literary fiction? And in a very real sense, who (aside from literary critic Harold Bloom) the hell cares? We either love it or hate it in the end, which is great, and perhaps the only failure, ultimately, is the work that leaves us indifferent. Similarly, we can take an acknowledged genre writer like Dennis Lehane, and ask why his works would necessarily lack any more of the beauty (or truth, or mythology) of art than those of [insert currently celebrated literary darling here]… And, like I say, I'm not even all that sure we can use "art" as a legitimate criterion or signpost here, anyway.

Indeed, there have been times in the history of English literature when the distinction was as plainly meaningless as I'm arguing here. Stories and storytelling were not politely revered in some airless grand hall, but were populist mass entertainment, gaudy and messy as medieval marketplaces, and this is nothing to be ashamed of. Without such street theatre, the single greatest practitioner of the written and spoken language, William Shakespeare, would probably not have emerged from his decidedly average education and lower middle class roots. Similarly, without the Bardic tradition of songs, poetry may not have evolved. Why would we wish to unravel all that—the music, the words, the rhythms, the art, the entertainment, the colourful cultural detritus both good and bad—so we can score meaningless points over something that ought not be a contest in the first place?

Perhaps language itself is the problem here. As in, we're using it wrongly. For the sake of argument, let's take science fiction as an example. There is hack science fiction and there is good science fiction. No one would argue this. Perhaps, therefore, we should be merging our terms and speaking of literary science fiction. In other words, if something is written well, its subject matter and even genre conventions become less important. Good, bad, indifferent. These are the only distinctions that matter. And quite honestly, I reserve more opprobrium for the latter than I do for the first two. I prefer full-on bad to bland and safe. But that's just me.

Anyway, apologies for getting all philosophical in this chapter—I certainly don't claim to have had the last word on this and may indeed revisit it in future, and welcome further thoughts, or even mass ridicule. Although, be gentle with me, I'm far more fragile than I look. But hey, in the interest of fairness, let's just say there's a hint of truth lurking within the distinction. In which case, we may give the last word to Stephen King (whose work has fallen into either category over the course of a long career), who memorably and respectfully summarized the difference between the two in a way that avoids any declaration of war:

"I have no quarrel with literary fiction which usually concerns itself with extraordinary people in ordinary situations, but as a reader and a writer, I'm much more interested in ordinary people in extraordinary situations." [From the Afterword, *Full Dark, No Stars*, 2010]

Chapter Sixteen: Hot And Fresh Out The Kitchen

Editing. Not a concept that fills most writers with joy. For many, it's the unpleasant yet necessary shadow accompanying the act of writing itself, sort of how a painful rash can follow a good, healthy... um, hike through poison ivy. And I see why many of us feel that way, I really do. Or I did. Lately, along with extra wrinkles around my eyes and greyer hair at my temples (okay, not just my temples, but we don't need to get all TMI, do we?), I've begun to appreciate editing for what it is. I'm not talking about the editing I do for others, necessarily, although I could be. No, I'm referring more to my own process in that regard. Something dawned on me: I'm starting to enjoy it. Now, either I am growing more masochistic than I ever believed possible, or my new realisation has actual substance. Again, for TMI-avoidance purposes, let's go with the latter.

Here, I'll just say it: editing is an integral part of the creative process and isn't really qualitatively different from writing. What we tend to call "writing" is in fact "initial drafting" and what we often think of as "editing" is just a deeper form of "writing". Every bit as creative, and potentially just as satisfying. At its best, it's the layers of paint over the pencil sketch. I realize there may be folks reading this who are kind of looking askance at me and thinking "no, duh, did you just receive your first clue via a Wells Fargo stagecoach?", and to those people I hold up my hands, guilty as charged: what others have perhaps known for a goodly while genuinely occurred to me, like, yesterday. Look, I'm a slow learner, okay, but at least I'm a learner.

So, what do I mean? Well, the best way to get something across is to demonstrate it, to literally show and not tell. So, I'll write a quick draft of a fabricated passage from a non-existent fantasy novel, here:

The men rode up the hill, the army of trolls behind them. They paused at the top and looked across a burning landscape, the distant city sending smoke high in the grey sky. Everything seemed hopeless. Ear'o'korn faced his men. "This is the moment. All paths have led to this. We must defeat our enemy or perish. Prepare the last stand of Condomia!" Stirred, the men renewed their faith and turned toward their pursuers, ready for battle again and prepared to fight to the last man for the Good and the Righteous.

Okay, I wrote that literally without pausing or second-guessing, which is how most of us either write or are told to write. In other words, bring on the heavy editing artillery long after the first draft, never during it. So, imagine I'm done my draft and am now returning to the passage in question for the first time. And I'm so not kidding, this part is fun. Either that, or I'm an incorrigible word nerd. Hmmm. Yeah, probably the latter. Oh, I should point out there is no one perfect way to edit such a passage; in fact, the possibilities are probably close to infinite, so don't attack my somewhat exaggerated style or you'll be missing the point (he says, covering his butt far too glibly).

Here's one way:

The men rode to the summit of the hill... I prefer this as it negates the need for "at the top" in the next sentence *...the troll army following.* Again, it feels more efficient and works better rhythmically. *Pausing amid a cloud of*

dust... This engages the senses, adds verisimilitude
...they looked out across a ravaged landscape, at the burned forests and the columns of smoke rising from the distant city. A little more description, just enough to conjure a scene, but allowing the reader to fill in some of the detail of what a ravaged landscape looks like.
Dismay and horror crossed their faces like shadows. This isn't great, but it's still better visually than "everything seemed hopeless". You could probably lose one of "dismay" or "horror" if you wanted it tighter.
Raising his voice, Ear'o'korn spoke. "Faced his men" is too Hollywood, too inorganic, he's in the middle of a disorganized, demoralized party of weary soldiers, after all, not giving a fresh battle speech at the outset of a conflict. *"Men, this is our moment to defeat despair. We have arrived here together, having traveled many paths. Two choices now remain: vanquish...* we used "defeat" far too recently, and it has a nice balance alongside the upcoming "perish" *...our enemy or perish in the attempt. In the name of all that's good, for the sake of all we hold dear, prepare the last stand of Condomia! Fight as the brothers we are!"* Sometimes we add words, sometimes we eliminate them. This is an example in which the passage requires more length, his speech needing to fit the "high speech" mold of epic fantasy, and rather than tell the readers his men were moved by it, we allow the words themselves to do the job, bolstered by a simple description afterward. *As he spoke, the soldiers grew taller in the saddle, slowly turning their horses to face their pursuers. Jaws set, weapons raised, they roared in unison, each man welcoming the final charge, the possibility of his own death.* Now, again, this isn't perfect or even great, but you get the idea that each time we lay down another layer or another shade of paint, we hope to improve the bigger picture. Of course, this leads to another huge question outside the purview of this

post: when do you stop? If you daub too many layers, you end up with a muddy, sloppy mess of words and a ruined picture. Anyway, for comparison purposes, I'll paste the edited version here.

The men rode to the summit of the hill, the troll army following. Pausing amid a cloud of dust, they looked out across a ravaged landscape, at the burned forests and the columns of smoke rising from the distant city. Dismay and horror crossed their faces like shadows. Raising his voice, Ear'o'korn spoke. "Men, this is our moment to defeat despair. We have arrived here together, having traveled many paths. Two choices now remain: vanquish our enemy or perish in the attempt. In the name of all that's good, for the sake of all we hold dear, prepare the last stand of Condomia! Fight as the brothers we are!" As he spoke, the soldiers grew taller in the saddle, slowly turning their horses to face their pursuers. Jaws set, weapons raised, they roared in unison, each man welcoming the final charge, the possibility of his own death.

Yeah, okay, still needs work. I kind of cheated, too, as this type of writing is almost built on cliché, so I didn't have to worry too much about that aspect, at least. But hopefully you get my bigger point, that this is writing every bit as creative and enjoyable as that first rough sketch, perhaps more so. That it's all part of the larger process. It's work, but it's also play.

Once again, an analogy from my other favourite art form—music—rides in like Ear'o'korn to rescue us at the death. Far from being drudgery, what we term editing is really a re-working, is in fact not so much an edit as a remix. And as such, it can be truly radical. If you're still skeptical, go track down R. Kelly's original

"Ignition", then listen to "Ignition: Remix". Clue: one is possibly the greatest song of the new Millennium, and the other... uh, isn't.

Chapter Seventeen: From Minds Profound

All over the internet, you can dig up articles and blog posts that establish writing rules as far from absolute, deeming them best interpreted as guides than anything more binding. But far more effective than a plainly stated rule is the aphorism, that memorable quote that both entertains and teaches... something. I keep a running list of quotes in general, but those pertaining to writing have pride of place, and they can alternately act as impetus or inspiration when you're flagging, as an alarm bell when you're off track, as a way to stay humble when you become overinflated, or simply as a way to laugh at yourself when you happen to forget how absurd you are. I present to you my **Top Twenty Awesome Writing Quotes**, mostly written by other writers, but remember: whatever germ of a lesson they contain, it's not a rule, okay?

20. "I once asked this literary agent what kind of writing paid the best. He said, 'Ransom notes.'" *Get Shorty* (1995) – Harry Zimm (Gene Hackman)

Money? I vaguely remember that stuff. It's green, I think. I swear, incidentally, that Gene Hackman gets some of the most gleefully brilliant lines in Hollywood. As Sheriff Daggett in *Unforgiven*, after being told he'd just beat the daylights out of an innocent man, he got to say this: "Innocent? Innocent of what?" To which there is quite simply no conceivable answer.

19. "A professional writer is an amateur who didn't quit." – Richard Bach

He wrote about a seagull. He said this. Succinct is this guy's middle name. Or wait, isn't it "Livingston"? No. No, that was the seagull.

18. "It is impossible to discourage the real writers – they don't give a damn what you say, they're going to write." – Sinclair Lewis

It's not a job, it's a calling. Like the urge to use the bathroom. If you feel that, Lewis is talking about you. The writing thing, not the bathroom thing.

17. "If you're going to be a writer, the first essential is just to write. Do not wait for an idea. Start writing something and the ideas will come. You have to turn the faucet on before the water starts to flow." – Louis L'Amour

What might have been a fairly ordinary, common sense platitude is rescued—like when the guy with the poncho and the sandblown crowsfeet rides into town—by a startlingly apt metaphor.

16. "I've been reading reviews of my stories for twenty-five years, and can't remember a single useful point in any of them, or the slightest good advice. The only reviewer who ever made an impression on me was Skabichevsky, who prophesied that I would die drunk in the bottom of a ditch." – Anton Chekhov

Um, only take the bad reviews to heart? No, that's not what Chekhov's saying here at all. I'm not really sure *what* he's saying, but it made me laugh anyway. Odd. I don't remember him being this funny in *Star Trek*.

15. "You must write your first draft with your heart. You rewrite with your head. The first key to writing is to write, not to think!" *Finding Forrester* (2000) – William Forrester (Sean Connery)

You won't go too far wrong if you remember this, while simultaneously forgetting Sean Connery ever starred in this clunky embarrassment of a movie.

14. "I'm all in favour of keeping dangerous weapons out of the hands of fools. Let's start with typewriters." – Frank Lloyd Wright

Okay, it's dated, but it's too good to exclude on that basis. If you must, substitute "laptops" or even "tablets" for the last word. Although, face it, the latter would sound weird.

13. "If my doctor told me I had only six minutes to live, I wouldn't brood. I'd type a little faster." – Isaac Asimov

He means it, too. You can just tell.

12. "There's no free lunch. Writing is work. It's also gambling. You don't get a pension plan. Other people can help you a bit, but essentially you're on your own. Nobody is making you do this: you chose it, so don't whine." – Margaret Atwood

Well, that told us. Wait, I didn't know that about the pension plan…

10. "To me, the greatest pleasure of writing is not what it's about, but the inner music the words make." – Truman Capote

Included here because I agree one hundred per cent. You don't have to, but it's my list.

9. "If you can't annoy somebody with what you write, I think there's little point in writing." – Kingsley Amis

Put more strongly than I'd put it, but then again, Amis was by all accounts a class one melonfarmer. I've always said, however, that you sure can't worry about offending people when you write. Unless you're *aiming* for anodyne, that is.

8. "I was working on the proof of one of my poems all the morning and took out a comma. In the afternoon, I put it back in." – Oscar Wilde

The sad part is, I get this. I know this. And I'll bet you do too. I'll also bet Wilde was tempted to remove that damn comma again by nightfall.

7. "What creates a writer is huge, psychological dysfunction." – Kathy Lette

Well, I've hinted at it here, before. Kathy Lette, however, just comes right out and *says* it. And it's kind of a horrible relief. Like when Asimov's doctor up there delivers the bad news. Like Isaac, we now know where we stand.

6. "Writing is easy. All you do is stare at a blank sheet of paper until drops of blood form on your forehead." – Gene Fowler

Easy, you say? Anyone else detect the sarcasm here?

5. "Poets need not go to Niagara to write about the force of falling water." – Robert Frost

Worth remembering. An antidote to "write what you know". There's a reason we have an imagination. But it takes a poet to say it so memorably and so well.

4. "Ever tried? Ever failed? No matter. Try again. Fail again. Fail better." – Samuel Beckett

And you thought Richard Bach was succinct? Also, why isn't the word "succinct" only one syllable? A question I am apparently compelled to return to like a killer to the scene of his crimes.

3. "The King died and then the Queen died. That is a story. The King died and then the Queen died of grief. That is a plot." – E. M. Forster

Brilliant. Since I like this kind of thing so much, I will throw in a bonus **3.b.:** "The cat sat on the mat is not a story. The cat sat on the other cat's mat is a story." – John le Carré

2. "Times are bad. Children no longer obey their parents and everyone is writing a book." – Cicero, *circa* 43 BC

All I know from this is that things don't change all that much and that Cicero would probably have a catastrophic mental breakdown if he lived today.

1. "Everywhere I go I'm asked if I think the university stifles writers. My opinion is that they don't stifle enough of them." – Flannery O'Connor

Ha ha. That one's a stand alone. Flannery sure doesn't need me to expand on it. Not that any of them do, really. But I had to write a chapter, so I have. Enjoy.

Or, as Dorothy Parker (who clearly didn't have Google and/or Text Edit handy) once said: "I might repeat to myself, slowly and soothingly, a list of quotations beautiful from minds profound; if I can remember any of the damn things."

Chapter Eighteen: Well Defined? Nevermind

Writers. We write. And our tools are words. So, while contemplating this week's chapter, I had the brilliant idea of writing about words and their definitions, using… words and their definitions. It's almost perfect. If by "perfect" I mean "utterly stupid and almost entirely pointless." (Which itself ought to be the title of a Jonathan Safran Foer novel.) So, anyway, a couple years ago, *The New York Times* compiled a list of the 50 words most likely to stump their own readers. Amazingly, "defenestrate" was not among them (if it had been, I would have defined it as "To demonstrate a specialty fencing technique often used to remove the fins of albacore tuna"). Unhelpfully, perhaps, they neglected to include definitions. Which is where I come in. Don't get me wrong—this being the internet which, like nature, abhors a vacuum—somebody already came along and performed this admirable service, but I'm going to go one better. I will proceed to pick 13 of the 50 words, more or less at random, and provide not one but two definitions, one of which is the correct one and one which I made up out of whole cloth for no other reason than to be extremely annoying. And if you're just as bored as me (woah, Cobain flash), you can follow along and expose me for the consummate liar I am. And since I'm also most likely stealing this whole idea from a board game or something, I'm a liar *and* a thief (lookit, another Cobain flash).

1. Nascent.

a) The act of saying no to the wearing of artificial fragrance. Smells like teen spirit? Uh-uh. Not a chance when we're being all nascent.
b) Just coming into existence and beginning to display signs of future potential.

2. Hubris.

a) Excessive pride.
b) A type of cheese rendered from human fat. Illegal in most countries.

3. Jejune.

a) While reciting the months of the year, "jejune" is the act of stammering inexplicably over the summer months (see also, "Jejuly").
b) Naïve, simple.

4. Profligacy.

a) Reckless extravagance; wastefulness.
b) The entire body of work left by an academic.

5. Austerity.

a) Sternness or severity of manner or attitude.
b) The quality of an upside down gaze, *chiefly Aus*. Was coined during the 1956 Melbourne Olympics by tourists attempting to capture the peculiar way Australians stared at them and their touristy Northern Hemisphere ways.

6. Solipsistic.

a) The slightly desperate and certainly reckless act of slipping your own sister a sedative to shut her up after a long day of her pointing out how badly you suck at life.
b) The view or theory that the self is all that can be known to exist.

7. Redoubtable.

a) Formidable, esp. as an opponent.
b) Something so ludicrously implausible that you will not only doubt it, but you will return and doubt it again.

8. Obstreperous.

a) Noisy and difficult to control.
b) Behaviour typical of a gynaecologist with a throat infection.

9. Sanguine.

a) A flightless bird from Antarctica that has been officially sanctified by the Vatican.
b) Optimistic or hopeful, especially in a bad situation.

10. Egregious.

a) Outstandingly bad; shocking.
b) An online lobbying group for men named Greg.

11. Polemicist.

a) A drug store employee native to Poland.
b) A person skilled in verbal or written attacks.

12. Hegemony.

a) Leadership or dominance of one country over another.
b) The unit of currency used in small hedgehog economies.

13. Feckless.

a) Lacking initiative or strength of character.
b) The baffling inability to use profanity in the country of Ireland.

I hope this was an enjoyable exercise for you all. Personally, since puns make me physically ill, I found it excruciating, but in the last words of someone who keeps spookily hijacking my article from beyond the grave: peace, love, empathy (the latter meaning "an illness brought on by exposure to the letter 'm'").

Chapter Nineteen: Armless and Legless

Our wonderful interwebs are full of blogs and writing websites that showcase an endless procession of writing advice and tips. I've discussed the pros and cons here in this odd little book many times, so I don't want to go over old ground. While planning the content of this chapter in the quiet small hours, however, it seemed like a good idea at the time to take a slightly skewed, bizarro-world look at writing tips using our trusty list format. Now, it seems… well, slightly stupid. But since I didn't have a backup, here it is, anyway: a new kind of list. **Twenty-Five Writing Tips That Probably Suck**. Seriously, though, I'm not wasting anyone's time: loosely hidden within this apparent drivel are some actual decent tips, once they're extricated and unpacked. You'll see.

1. Understatement is absolutely essential. Without it, you're dead in the water. In fact, there's no hope whatsoever.

2. Avoid semicolons; they're just not necessary.

3. The complete avoidance of passive clauses is very much advised by me.

4. Weather ewe think your aloud two ore knot … always rely on you're spellchecker.

5. Eschew ostentatious verbosity, and exhibit an overall predisposition toward a paucity of embellishment.

6. Eighty-six dialect unless yer lugholes are mint, yo.

7. If you inject opinion, I think you should be struck from the author's list, skewered on a buck elk's rack during rutting season, and parboiled in liquefied hamster entrails.

8. Over-explaining can lead to a kind of paralysis on the part of the reader, during which their mental processes become overloaded and, in a classic demonstration of diminishing returns, become less able to absorb the full import of your writing, which behooves you to restrict exposition to a minimum, when all is said and done.

9. *Entre nous,* while foreign languages are awesome, *au courant bon mots* may appear excessive if they become *de rigeur,* and may even invite *schadenfreude,* so *caveat emptor,* and try to avoid this type of *mea culpa* or *faux pas, comprende?*

10. Omit, pare and cull entirely redundant, superfluous and needless words.

11. Pay great attention, to how you use punctuation.

12. As I once thought-spoke to that gelatinous glob of alien protoplasm from Arcturus over a pint of fermented gerbil spleens, write what you know!

13. Do not use commas, to bracket phrases, that are essential to a sentence's meaning.

14. Never let someone else edit edit your own work; it's you're baby, and besides, you don't know wear they've been.

15. Stop!! Think about the overuse of exclamation points!!

16. Make hay while the iron's hot and don't mix your metaphors.

17. My impression is that it's probably not the best idea to be sort of vague about stuff.

18. Make sure your grammar works good.

19. Always finish what you

20. Do not construct gobsmackingly, facemeltingly awkward adverbs.

21. Do not misuse apostrophe's.

22. In dialogue, be sure the reader knows who's speaking, said the Dalai Lama.

23. Avoid tired clichés like the plague. When you notice one in your writing, hone in on your target and deep six it with extreme prejudice.

24. A while back, right over there someplace, I was talking to some guy about this one: be specific with details.

25. As Orwell once said, only to immediately break his own rule: "never use a metaphor, simile, or other figure of speech which you are used to seeing in print." George, dude, you were awesome and stuff, but isn't "figure of speech" itself a, um, figure of speech?

I kid, of course. Orwell knew what he was talking about. Otherwise, how else would he have teamed up with that Rickenbacker dude to invent popcorn? And now, as a treat for wading through my inanities, here's another guy (http://www.youtube.com/watch?v=VyQ1wEBx1V0) who actually knew what he was talking about, so much so that he once said "When I write, I feel like an armless, legless man with a crayon in his mouth." Exactly. Now he's the type of guy you need to listen to. Not me, him. Sadism and cockroaches notwithstanding.

Chapter Twenty: My God, it's Full of Stars!

For this chapter, I'm going to be a little more serious than usual. No idea why. I just am. And I want to talk about star ratings. No, I don't want to discuss the relative merits of Justin Bieber or Katy Perry, fascinating as that might be; I'm talking about the graded star method many websites use to rate various products, but specifically as it pertains to indie authors, that aspect of the review system used by the mighty Amazon.

Sometimes feeling like I've accidentally wandered into a cosmologist convention, I keep hearing my fellow writers discussing star systems, conversations that range from the alleged importance of 5-Star ratings to dire warnings of the career damage caused by 1-Star ratings. There are even dark tales of jealous authors deliberately dropping a single star on the book pages of their competitors... a frankly bizarre behaviour, if true, since my admittedly collectivist-hippie-skewed moral compass informs me we're less competitors than we are colleagues. My favourite star-related content is M. Edward McNally's regular inclusion of 1-Star customer ratings for classic novels. The ratings, along with their concomitant cluelessness (or, arguably, fresh perspectives), are hilarious.

But let's back up for a moment... as the actress said to the... oh, wait. No. Serious, remember? When I started writing music reviews for *PopMatters*, a large and very eclectic online pop culture magazine, unlike other similar outlets at the time, we didn't do number ratings. I liked that. We were encouraged to really delve into the guts of whatever we were reviewing, blending journalistic facts with a more personal exploration of the music. I don't regret my time writing for them one little bit. At the time, I was reading the thoughts of other music writers, many of whom debated the purpose of reviews: some arguing they were basically consumer guides and others championing the so-called "think piece" aspects of the form, and everything in between. If you're interested, Robert Christgau is a great proponent and practitioner of the former (he literally names his reviews dating back to 1969 "Consumer Guides"), while the latter would probably be best personified by the late Lester Bangs (if you haven't read him, do so, he's great). Greil Marcus, too.

Now, I won't claim I stopped writing for the site on any regular basis *solely* due to their introduction of number ratings, but I'm sure it was a factor when I decided to move on. They honestly felt arbitrary. Was my job to grade or rate, or was it to explore? Some might say both, and I've some sympathy with that position, but regardless, my own emphasis was very much on the latter. Why did it matter what number I assigned? Surely, the exploration of my reactions to the music, maybe some insight into the music's roots or influences, comparisons with similar artists, were more valuable than a numerical rating… otherwise, why bother with the written review at all? I've never subscribed to the view, incidentally, that sees critics as failed artists, as something parasitic or even malicious. Oh, sure, some of them can be—music writing in particular can often be damn near toxic with snark—but at its best, the great review is complementary to the art it describes or eulogizes. It can and ought to be a symbiotic relationship.

So Amazon is in the business of selling books. They know the consumer likes to see a product quantified, so star ratings make sense for them. But for me—and I know I'm not completely alone in this—I want to hear about someone's emotional engagement with a work. I want to know how it made them feel, what other things it reminded them of, whether plot- or character-driven, whether the language was robust or fragile, pretty or brutal. The last thing I really care about is some fairly arbitrary star ratings. Because they *are* arbitrary. I've heard writers complain about a 3-Star rating they just had, which suggests they think it means the book is considered mediocre. For what it's worth, if forced at gunpoint to care, I'd make a comparison to the movie review aggregator Rotten Tomatoes, whereby a 60% rating is considered Fresh (as opposed to Rotten). Now, my math skills are as rudimentary as the reasoning abilities of a recently-defenestrated pygmy hedgehog, but even I can work out that 3 Stars is... uh ... 60%. Right?

All of which is my roundabout way of saying: don't sweat the numbers, read the reviews themselves—at their best, they're far more crucial to an understanding of whether you will enjoy a work or not. And my fellow indie authors, unless you strongly suspect malice (and Amazon will remove reviews that are demonstrably vindictive or spiteful), try to ignore the numerical aspect of the review and really get to grips with the words themselves. They're our stock-in-trade, after all, or we'd all be accountants instead. And, yeah, probably a lot richer.

Chapter Twenty-One: Build Your Wings

When I was maybe 12 or 13 years old, one of the first stories I ever wrote was about an old man wandering the streets in a dystopian future. He was so old and forgotten that he couldn't even remember his name, going by the initials RDB. Those initials, of course, stood for Raymond Douglas Bradbury, and the man at the time was my literary hero. My very obvious stylistic mimicry of him back then, in that and many other proto-stories, was excruciating yet necessary; all part of a writer's journey. But it's no exaggeration to say I almost certainly wouldn't have been a writer had it not been for Ray Bradbury and his short stories in particular. Up until the time I opened a well-pawed library copy of *The Illustrated Man*, I knew I loved stories (what kid doesn't?), but I'd never realised until that moment how those stories could be presented, enclosed in beauty, garnished with lyricism and beauty. Not just the tale but the telling. That was Bradbury's gift to me and countless other readers who, thanks to his example, also began to dream of being writers.

In some ways it would be churlish to lament the passing of a man who lived to the grand age of 91. Yet in others, his talent was so immense, the legacy he leaves so comprehensive—his longevity itself somehow becoming a part of that legacy—that I have to admit to a great sadness at his passing this year.

In terms of politics and overall cultural views, it would be difficult to find a public figure I disagreed with less yet admired more than Mr. Bradbury. But then again, he always was a contradiction: a science fiction pioneer who mistrusted hard science, a visionary for a brighter future who disliked technology, a starfield dreamer who set much of his work in small-town Illinois (you could say his Green Town was the antecedent of Stephen King's Castle Rock). In one sense, he was a conservative neo-Luddite. Yet in others, he was a compassionate and populist advocate for creativity and the arts and the restless, rebellious spirit.

But this won't be a long tribute. In fact, I'm going to let the man himself have his say for the most part. The following are thirteen choice quotes in no particular order, after which I will include two short passages from two of his short stories that, in some ways, best sum up the exuberance and wonder of this great American writer. He wrote horror, he wrote science fiction, he wrote fantasy. But far more importantly, he wrote.

1. "You don't have to burn books to destroy a culture. Just get people to stop reading them."

2. "People ask me to predict the future, when all I want to do is prevent it. Better yet, build it."

3. "My stories run up and bite me in the leg — I respond by writing down everything that goes on during the bite. When I finish, the idea lets go and runs off."

4. "The good writers touch life often. The mediocre ones run a quick hand over her. The bad ones rape her and leave her for the flies."

5. "Stuff your eyes with wonder. Live as if you'd drop dead in ten seconds. See the world. It's more fantastic than any dream made up or paid for in factories."

6. "I have never listened to anyone who criticized my taste in space travel, sideshows or gorillas. When this occurs, I pack up my dinosaurs and leave the room."

7. "Science fiction is the most important literature in the history of the world."

8. "Science fiction balances you on the cliff. Fantasy shoves you off."

9. "We are cups, constantly and quietly being filled. The trick is knowing how to tip ourselves over and let the beautiful stuff out."

10. "Every morning I jump out of bed and step on a landmine. The landmine is me. After the explosion, I spent the rest of the day putting the pieces together."

11. "If you hide your ignorance, no one will hit you and you'll never learn."

12. "We are the miracle of force and matter making itself over into imagination and will. Incredible. The Life Force experimenting with forms. You for one. Me for another. The Universe has shouted itself alive. We are one of the shouts."

13. "Go to the edge of the cliff and jump off. Build your wings on the way down."

*

An example of his astonishing descriptive abilities and feel for language first, his visceral and poetic sensibility. Here is Bradbury describing a Tyrannosaurus Rex in his famous story "A Sound of Thunder."

"It came on great oiled, resilient, striding legs. It towered thirty feet above half of the trees, a great evil god, folding its delicate watchmaker's claws close to its oily reptilian chest. Each lower leg was a piston, a thousand pounds of white bone, sunk in thick ropes of muscle, sheathed over in a gleam of pebbled skin like the mail of a terrible warrior. Each thigh was a ton of meat, ivory, and steel mesh [...] And the head itself, a ton of sculptured stone, lifted easily upon the sky. Its mouth gaped, exposing a fence of teeth like daggers. Its eyes rolled, ostrich eggs, empty of all expression save hunger. It closed its mouth in a death grin."

And sometimes, he was able to capture something beyond wistfulness and dreams, something both timeless and in the moment, the sweep of human history measured against the capacity for human yearning and, well, love. This, from a short story called "The Wilderness":

"Is this how it was over a century ago, she wondered, when the women, the night before, lay ready for sleep, or not ready, in the small towns of the East, and heard the sound of horses in the night and the creak of the Conestoga wagons ready to go, and the brooding of oxen under the trees, and the cry of children already lonely before their time? All the sounds of arrivals and departures into the deep forests and fields, the blacksmiths working in their own red hells through midnight? And the smell of bacons and hams ready for the journeying, and the heavy feel of the wagons like ships foundering with goods, with water in the wooden kegs to tilt and slop across prairies, and the chickens hysterical in their slung-beneath-the-wagon crates, and the dogs running out to the wilderness ahead and,

93

fearful, running back with a look of empty space in their eyes? Is this, then, how it was so long ago? On the rim of the precipice, on the edge of the cliff of stars. In their time the smell of buffalo, and in our time the smell of the Rocket. Is this, then, how it was?

"And she decided, as sleep assumed the dreaming for her, that yes, yes indeed, very much so, irrevocably, this was as it had always been and would forever continue to be."

Chapter Twenty-Two: Phoque It

Note to staff: This is an early draft of a sales pitch. Please correct and edit before release. Under no circumstances should this be allowed to see the light of day in its current state.

Dear readers, writers, book industry people,

It's become a cliché to claim there's a veritable Pacific Ocean of crapola out there in the indie book world. But that cliché is not even a good analogy, really, so we're going to turn it on its head. No, instead of an ocean, what we see is a vast floating island of ugly unbiodegradable plastic that grows vaster and uglier by the day. It's at least as ugly as the word "unbiodegradable". And we want to clean it up. Now, is there anything living in the ocean we can all get behind? Excluding those mean, club-wielding Canadians, that is? ~~Wait, club-wielding Canadians are aquatic?~~ Seals, of course!

With their large innocent eyes, playful natures and smooth, round torsos, pretty much everyone adores ~~Canadians~~ seals. Since we all approve of seals, it makes sense you will want to pay me to stamp your book with the "seal" of "approval" (clever, huh?). And since the French for seal is "phoque", our company's name almost writes itself: Phoque It. Geddit? It's almost too perfect. Don't know about you, but I'm giddy already.

So, here is my proposal. I have formed a collective. Right now it's just me, admittedly, but my multiple personalities do actually qualify me in this ~~lowdown~~

~~masquerade~~ exciting new venture. Anyway, I am going to ~~fleece~~ help all of you. And here's how. Pretty much everyone agrees that indie books are somewhat quality-challenged, yeah? ~~Quite honestly, I've seen better-written grocery lists than some of these so-called ebooks. Somewhere there's a monkey sitting at a typewriter with more talent in one knuckle of its left pinkie finger than most of these losers.~~ But what if we had a way to guarantee quality? You then get happy readers, of course. Who suddenly ~~stop wanting to douse indies in grain alcohol and flambé them on a barbecue while cursing in an ancient Maori dialect~~ start to drop their criticisms of indie authors. And who then buy more books written by said indies. After which, the collective self esteem index rises. Thus ensuring everyone wins. It's the mother of all positive feedback loops. ~~And with absolutely no more flambéing.~~

Look, I'll cut to the chase: I have now patented a top-secret algorithm that can objectively evaluate the quality of any book. It took the best part of two years and the ~~illegal abduction~~ expert help of a number of prominent scientists from MIT to create this unique software, but now you can benefit from its 100% accuracy. Not only is it able to assess grammatical accuracy, it can also rate such previously unquantifiable aspects of the writer's craft as narrative arc, plot holes, the overuse of exposition, even a precarious imbalance of tell over show.

Once evaluated objectively by the program, our panel of industry experts will then pore over your work in order to provide that human touch. If ~~I~~ they decree it to be a reasonable standard, they will issue the Bronze Phoque to wear with pride on your book cover, and you will ~~fork over~~ pay the collective the incredibly low price of $250.

The Silver Phoque is reserved for slightly more elevated works, in which the dialogue is perhaps a little tighter, the language more tonally consistent, and we still only charge the almost painfully low rate of $350. Painful for us, I must emphasize. ~~You, on the other hand, will feel an almost unbearable pleasurable sensation in your nether regions when you cheerfully part with such a paltry sum.~~

Finally, the Gold Phoque will demonstrate to everyone the bewitching, beguiling brilliance of your book, will suffuse it with—yes—golden lambent light and the mellifluous tones of otherworldly choirs (as well as the large Gold Phoque so prominently displayed on your book's cover for the whole world to admire), all for the astonishingly, ~~damn near embarrassingly~~ low price of $500.

We even tested our amazing system on a bona fide classic, with somewhat surprising results. Awarding *To Kill a Mockingbird* a Bronze Phoque, the software had this to say: "A bit weighty for a YA novel. This, alongside some disturbing displays of racism, frankly, prevents this book from achieving a higher rating from our literat-o-meter. We would encourage the author to find less offensive subject matter in light of the young age and impressionability of the novel's protagonist". It also suggested Shakespeare go back and rewrite his stuff in "a language we can all understand." Okay, so there may be a few minor glitches and bugs to be worked out, but I can assure you of this: your book will be in expert hands. What can possibly go wrong?

This is the next step in our adventure together, my avid indie fleet. We are shedding gatekeepers like a squid sheds ink. Today we have set sail toward an unknown land. There may well be hungry sharks and heavy storms along the way. Pirates, even. But we are going to kill with righteous fury that ugly island of plastic, we're going to remake our ocean voyage in our image, and we're going to do it with seals, by imbuing them with approval, by showing we care only for quality and not stupid money, which you can't take with you anyway. What are a few pennies when placed beside immortality, after all? I'll answer that for you. Nothing, is what they are.

Which reminds me: here's my last word, since you now know my word is good. In order to further cement your trust, we will demonstrate our exemplary self-marketing competence by providing one of the industry's more memorable slogans:

"Here at Phoque It, You Give Us Money, Then We Give A Phoque."

Thank you for your time.

Chapter Twenty-Three: A Cautionary Tale About Cautionary Tales?

While discussing the great nation of Scotland recently, I was reminded of something. Undoubtedly, Scotland has bestowed upon our world some fine gifts, including the telephone, television, penicillin, caber tossing, Billy Connolly, the Glasgow Kiss, the Bay City Rollers and the words "bampot", "stoater", "drookit", "hackit" and "blootered". (I discern a visit to the Urban Dictionary in your future, dear reader.)

But along with such distinguished cultural contributions, Scotland also produced the mother of all cautionary tales, a tale that exemplifies supreme "bathos" (no, silly, Bathos isn't the name of the fourth Musketeer… and stop interrupting). And that tale goes by the name of William Topaz McGonagall. (Yes, I did just say "Topaz". Bear with me, you'll see.)

First, bathos. Here's the dictionary definition:

bathos |bāTHäs|
noun
(esp. in a work of literature) an effect of anticlimax created by an unintentional lapse in mood from the sublime to the trivial or ridiculous.

The key word there is "unintentional". For some unaccountable reason, something already funny is far funnier when it isn't meant to be. If you doubt me, think back to your school days when you were passed a note featuring a crude rendition of a specific body part, and at that moment the teacher uttered the terrible words,

"David, please share with the class what you clearly find so amusing." (Yes, I know your name isn't David, you're missing my point, keep up. Sigh.) Anyway, the effect was excruciating. Your internal organs would seem to liquefy, then inexplicably feel like gravity had just increased tenfold. Your hands would sweat, your face take on the texture and hue of something you'd order from Domino's. There would be a feeling in your throat somewhat akin to having a nest of boll weevils stuffed in your trachea, aching for release. Bottom line: forbidden humour is simply funnier.

So, who was William McGonagall? Well, he was a poet. Of sorts. More accurately, he was a truly abominable poet. If he was in any other field, not even the most militant union could have saved his job. But the spectacular part is that he believed he was gifted... and not only with verse. He also acted. So filled with hubris was this man that while playing the role of Macbeth, he once refused to die at the appointed moment in the play. I suppose rewriting Shakespeare on the fly is a form of subverted genius. Who knows what went on in this man's head?

There are so many examples of his execrable poetry out there in Google-land (he wrote some 200+ of the things), so I'll just drop a quote from the conclusion of his most famous poem, "The Tay Bridge Disaster". Keep in mind this is a lament for a very real disaster in which 75 people met horrible deaths when the Tay Rail Bridge near Dundee collapsed while a train was passing over it. Remember, we should not be laughing in any way at this...

> "Oh! Ill-fated bridge of the silv'ry Tay
> I now must conclude my lay

By telling the world fearlessly without the least dismay
That your central girders would not have given way
At least many sensible men do say
Had they been supported on each side with buttresses
At least many sensible men confesses
For the stronger we our houses build
The less chance we have of being killed."

A purer example of bathos we'd be hard pressed to find.

Oh, the Topaz part of his name? He once received a letter claiming to be from King Thibaw Min of Burma, informing him he'd been knighted as Sir Topaz, Knight of the White Elephant of Burmah. Either choosing to ignore or actually oblivious to this pretty obvious hoax, he henceforth referred to himself in his promotional material as "Sir William Topaz McGonagall, Knight of the White Elephant, Burmah". Can someone hoax me something along similar lines so I can start a Facebook page entitled, "Sir David Emerald Antrobus, Knight of the Gold Phoque, Cascadia", please?

Seriously, Google his name and I guarantee you will be helpless with laughter at many of the absurdities scattered throughout this man's life. Unaware or unconcerned as McGonagall himself was, some of the events surrounding his seventy-seven years on planet Earth are scarcely believable. Before I finish, I'll offer you one such tidbit. No one can argue the truth contained in his first "review", an ostensibly admiring comment from the subject of his very first poem, the Reverend George Gilfillan, who gushed, "Shakespeare never wrote anything like this." Quite.

But what does his example teach us, as we each try to make our way in this world of letters? Should we mock him or admire him? In a way, perhaps both. Certainly on one level, I'm actually envious of the man's stalwart self-belief. I'm as riddled with self doubt about my writing, after all, as the England national football team are about their continued progression at major tournaments: I just know I'm going out at the next penalty shootout. Whereas the McGonagalls of the world are apparently oblivious to those long dark tea-times of the soul (thank you, Douglas Adams), those quiet moments of reflection wherein most of us conclude our future most likely lies at a busy intersection holding a cardboard sign in one hand and a small, trembling dog in the other. But it's easy to snipe, and perhaps this cautionary tale conceals another level of caution altogether. Despite his almost complete lack of writing talent, McGonagall's bullheaded refusal to allow even a shred of self doubt to divert him from his vocation, his unerring insistence on his own brilliance, has ensured his seven collections of poetry are still being read over a hundred years after his death. Which, okay, is unintentionally funny, for sure, yet not really all that bathetic, is it?

Chapter Twenty-Four: Use Your Imagination

One of the earliest pieces of writing advice I ever remember reading arrived courtesy of Stephen King. It was three simple (if marginally crude) words: "ass in chair." Okay, fine. Thanks for that, Stephen. It can't be argued with, though. But the next question occurs once you have molded said body part firmly onto the furniture in question: how do you keep it there? How do you stay motivated and focused enough to type out the allotted number of words at whatever rate you've set yourself? Well, this week I thought I'd be helpful and share five simple techniques to keep you in your seat, facing your screen, typing mindlessly into a document. An activity we mystifyingly insist on calling "writing".

1. Remember the scene in *Lethal Weapon 2* where Danny Glover is sitting on the toilet and a bomb is wired to explode if he gets up off the seat? Well, there's a real clue to our dilemma right there. I don't mean boobytrap your computer chair with an actual bomb, although that would work too, I suppose. Albeit a tad risky. But no, we don't have to recreate it literally; I mean, we can let ourselves imagine a bomb going off if we stand up before our word quota is met, right? We are writers, after all. With imaginations, presumably. Oh, never mind.

2. So, you're quietly seething because all your friends took off for a day of sun and surf and you're sitting alone in this dingy basement again. How do you resist the urge to join them? Simple. With an unhealthy dose of *schadenfreude*, that's how. You tell yourself those selfsame frolicking, carefree friends will all lose ten years off their lives thanks to the malignant melanomas that were hatched in their ruined skin cells on this very day. You made the right call, and not only did you write your allotted number of words, but you will be healthier than everyone you know (as long as you ignore the impact on your health of lengthy periods of sedentary existence punctuated only by the rustle of a chip bag or the uncorking of another bottle of Cabernet).

3. You steadily release these literary masterpieces into the black hole of the mighty 'Zon. You then pointedly ignore the unanimous silence of the world's cruel indifference. In the movie that runs in your head, the one in which you are the star of course, you watch excitedly as your genius is acknowledged by the literati; you are now lauded among the greats. Okay, if you are able to ignore reality this remarkably, it isn't any great leap to further pretend there is a man with a hefty cheque waiting for you if you only finish this chapter, edit that section, proofread this paragraph. Add as many zeros to said cheque as you like. Hell, spell it "check", even, I don't care. Make the man a famous celebrity. Have him place a Care Bear in a headlock for no apparent reason. Make him laugh at sly librarians. It's your scenario. Self-delusion (along with near-psychosis) is an essential part of being a writer.

4. Tell yourself if you don't meet today's word quota, not only will you make the baby Jesus cry, but you will plunge a battalion of the adorablest kittens into a chronic depression that will eliminate the will to live for 38% of them. You want that on your conscience? (Wait, my spellcheck didn't flag "adorablest"? Has the world gone mad?)

5. And finally, if the other techniques fail, buy an industrial staple gun, around twenty tubes of Crazy Glue, a roll of the ever-handy duct tape, and use them in ways that will become obvious on even the most cursory of reflections to affix your rebel carcass to your chair.

Chapter Twenty-Five: Take Off, Eh?

I've read some interesting debates online recently pertaining to the differences between UK and US English. A while ago, Indies Unlimited's Stephen Hise highlighted the differences between the two Englishes when it involves the punctuation surrounding dialogue. Boy (George), do people take this stuff seriously. As well they should, though—our wondrous English language is as essential to us writers as pickled sheep's eyes dipped in fruit bat guano are to pregnant women. Utterly indispensable. But I ain't going there. Neither pregnant women nor the Limey/Yank debate, nosiree. Not even fruit bats. No, I want to talk today about a different type of English, and one that oftentimes gets completely overlooked in these discussions: Canadian English.

Let me begin with a story. When I first arrived in this vast, slightly bewildered country from England in the late '80s, I quickly found work in a group home for abused/neglected teens. Back then, I'm mildly ashamed to say, I smoked. A lot. Cigarettes, mostly (but I didn't inhale, I swear). So, one evening I was involved in a stressful situation dealing with a kid who was flipping out about something or other, and once calm had returned, I said (ostensibly to myself, but for some reason the words emerged as out-loud speech instead of innermost thoughts... no doubt my first mistake), "Boy, could I use a fag right about now." All of a sudden, I had the rapt and wary attention of every teenager in that home. You could have cut the silence with a great big silence cutter (I was far lazier with my metaphors back then). They stared. I stared back. Someone laughed nervously and said "duuuude" under his breath. In that shaky skateboarder voice—you know the one. Now, don't get me wrong, it ought to go without saying that the humour of this moment isn't at the expense of gay people, it's at the expense of a stupid, bigoted word alongside my own naivety and the propensity of adolescents to tend toward the homophobic. A perfect storm of awkwardness, really.

A related story, set in the same location, involved an evening in which I was helping another kid with her homework and needed to erase something (back when there were, uh, exercise books and pencils and, I don't know, quill pens dipped in squid bile and stuff). It was some difficult math problem and I knew I was in over my head, so after getting further frustrated by everyone's apparent indifference, I announced to anyone unfortunate enough to be in earshot, "Trying to help Sally here, guys, but I really need a rubber."

Silence again.

People giving me that Heath Ledger as The Joker face.

Then general ridicule.

You get the idea. We (sundry English speakers) walk a common road, but it really behooves ("behoves" in the UK, and I'm not even kidding) us to know the many points at which it forks before we stumble so far along Laughingstock Avenue we can't ever find our way back and die of an increasingly common disease known as *humiliatus lexichosis*.

So what is Canadian English? To answer that question, and purely for the purposes of illustration, I am going to use over-emphasis and exaggeration right now and demonstrate it by picking a group of sentences no sane person, Canadian or otherwise, would ever speak. The following paragraph is pretty much un-Canadian (which means it hates hockey and loves Prime Minister Harper) and the one after that is a frankly absurd Canadian translation:

So this annoying person walks into my apartment with a case of beer and a bottle of rum from Newfoundland, removes his beanie hat and says "go away, please." Sitting on the couch, I finish my Canadian bacon and suck on my ice pop, take a large swallow of soda, while thrusting one hand into the pocket of my hoodie and extracting a pair of dollar coins. "No need to be so hostile, my friend. Why not put on your athletic shoes and go grab us a couple of donuts? And while you're at it, go check the rain gutters, the garbage disposal and make sure the electricity is working." He retorts, "Only two dollars? You keep short-changing me I'll end up on employment insurance. Besides, it's quite a distance." "Don't get your panties in a bunch, it's only about a mile. Get back and let's party, okay?" "Cool, I guess." "Awesome."

Translated into "Canadian":

So this hoser walks into my bachelor with a two-four of brewskis and a two-six of Newfie screech, loses the toque and says "take off, eh?" Sitting on the chesterfield, I finish my back bacon and suck on my freezie, chug on my pop bottle, while thrusting my hand into the pocket of my bunny hug and fishing out a couple loonies. "Take a pill, eh. Grab your runners and pick us up a couple jam busters from Timmy's. And while you're at it, go check the eavestroughs, the garburator and

make sure the hydro's on." He says, "Two loons? You keep this up, I'll be collecting pogey. Besides, it's a ways away." "Nah, don't get your ginch in a knot, it's only a couple klicks. Get back soon and let's be giv-n-r."
"Skookum." "Beauty."

Of course, that is silly (some of these colloquialisms are regionalisms, and sadly, a few appear to be dying altogether). But then, Canada is a silly country. How else do you explain or describe a nation that takes hockey and beavers more seriously than, uh, wars and stuff? Other than "refreshingly peaceful", that is? Plus, we can never fully decide which English we're going to adopt. Along with the Brits, we will write "cheque" for "check", "centre" for "center", "colour" for "color", etc., but will also use "truck" instead of "lorry", "gas(oline)" instead of "petrol" and "tire" instead of "tyre". Most of us will pronounce Z as "zed" not "zee", which always backfires anti-climactically when we get to the very end of "The Alphabet Song" and find it no longer rhymes. So, in a very simplistic way, we've basically merged UK and US English and come up with our own hybrid, picking our allegiances apparently at random. A perfect example would be the suffixes *-ice* and *-ise*. For the noun, we sometimes adopt the British version (licence) while for the verb we follow the American (license). Except when we don't: for some nouns, we sometimes adopt the American version (practice) while for the verb we lean toward(s) the British (practise). And yet, where the Brits use *-ise*, we tend more and more to follow the American *-ize*. Once you realize it's a minefield, to be honest, you're ready for any *surprise*. Or… *Hize*. Okay, I think I broke something inside my head just then.

But anyway, despite our apparent vacillation between and reliance upon the two great influencers, we still manage to retain over 2,000 words that are unique to Canada. Words like "butter tart" (a small pastry tart), "poutine" (fries, gravy and cheese curds… the most delicious cardiac arrest you'll ever taste), "cheezies" (a curly cheese snack), "timbits" (small doughnut holes—note spelling—from Tim Horton's), "deke" (a move involving faking out an opposition player, originally in hockey), "parkade" (multilevel parking lot) and "washroom" (bathroom, toilet, restroom), etc. Phrases like "drop the gloves", which essentially means getting serious, preparing to fight, are once again derived from hockey, as is "puck bunny", a hockey groupie (sensing a theme here?). And even the word "hoser" itself, popularized (popularised?) by Bob and Doug McKenzie on SCTV's "The Great White North" segments, may itself refer to the tradition whereby the losing hockey team had to hose off the ice rink after a game. Although mainly a novelty/joke word in this form, we do actually use the verb "to hose", as in "broken", or even as in "to get wasted": "I hit a moose and now my car's hosed", "that sucks, let's go get hosed."

So, the moral of this story? Be aware of other forms of English. It will save you much potential embarrassment. If you're an American or Canadian in the UK, you really don't want to say something like "I tripped over and landed on my fanny" (unless you want them to think you're a contortionist), while an English person visiting North America would be ill-advised to express their surprise with the words, "well, blow me!" Well, unless…. never mind. And if any Canadian ever tells you he's been performing obscenities with canines, please know he's actually saying he's been slacking at work, no more no less.

Chapter Twenty-Six: The Mirror's Gaze

"Here is a list of terrible things,
The jaws of sharks, a vulture's wings,
The rabid bite of the dogs of war,
The voice of one who went before,
But most of all the mirror's gaze,
Which counts us out our numbered days."
— Clive Barker, *Days of Magic, Nights of War*

***

I did promise in an earlier chapter that I'd return to the theme of horror fiction, undoubtedly my favourite genre. As a result, this somewhat horror-related article will be lacking the lighthearted humour of my usual fare, so please skip this if you're not in the mood for heavy and ponderous (you can't even imagine how much I wanted to add a "LOL" at the end of that sentence).

It's going to be frankly impossible for me to write this chapter effectively or accurately unless I come clean about certain autobiographical facts, or full disclosures, or whatever journalistic convention dictates they're referred to as. For anyone who has read my first book, this won't exactly come as a shock. For, existing somewhere in the mostly buried and certainly haphazard detritus of my personal history is a barely legible doctor's note (aren't they all?), diagnosing me as suffering from Post Traumatic Stress Disorder and clinical depression. Now, here and elsewhere, it's been endlessly discussed and largely established that creativity tends to be accompanied by emotional and mental turmoil, so I'm not going to recross that familiar ground this time around, fascinating though it is.

No, I want to address something else. I belong to numerous online writers' groups, from Facebook to LinkedIn, and I am noticing a recurring question that frequently gets asked by novice writers, but perhaps surprisingly, not *solely* by novice writers. Usually presented in a tentative manner, it basically asks whether certain painful topics are off limits, whether writers ought to refrain—through simple good taste, perhaps, or more worryingly, as a duty toward readers' sensibilities?—from discussing certain painful aspects of the human condition, or even whether writers should avoid certain *words* (to me, the latter is akin to asking a painter to ignore specific colours). Now, I generally avoid these conversations, as I literally don't have the time to indulge in the lengthy handwringing that almost inevitably follows. And, quite honestly, I am not partial to being misjudged, as so often occurs on all sides when this topic is raised. So, in place of my usual silence in those conversations, here's a placeholder for my views on this, henceforth to be considered my definitive position. After which, you have my permission to go do something a lot more fun than reading my tortured and over-earnest opinionating.

So, what of those opinions? In one sense, they're simple: censorship, even self-censorship, is anathema to a writer. Anxiety and second-guesswork over the reception of anything you create will only shackle and smother you. Write the book you want to read—even if zombie gnomes, electric can openers, and baby nuns feature heavily—and damn the torpedoes. Now, obviously, I'm not talking about children's books, here; fluffy bunnies drenched in gore and cursing like inebriated sailors is never a good look. Well, hmmm… at least in that context it isn't. But let's assume we're talking about adults writing for adults. In which case, I don't think anything should be off the table. And I mean anything. Some of the best and sharpest writing I've read has refused to pull its punches in this regard, from Clive Barker's *Books of Blood* to Thomas Harris's *Silence of the Lambs* to Cormac McCarthy's *Blood Meridian* to Alice Sebold's *The Lovely Bones* to Jack Ketchum's *The Girl Next Door*. These books deal with cannibalism, cruelty, murder/rape, madness, child abuse and serial murder. Not exactly pleasant stuff. They are definitely upsetting. But are they well written? Do they stand comparison with other good or even great literature? Would I recommend them? Absolutely, yes to all of the above. The thing is (and not that this should matter, either): all evidence points to the fact that these authors are well-adjusted, generous, and compassionate people. Stephen King himself, who once wrote about a man who literally ate himself, is a wonderful human being, by all accounts. Conflating their subject matter with their personalities is as wrong-headed as inferring Shakespeare was a sadist (or a racist!) for describing Iago's treatment of Othello. Or for assuming that Marshall Mather's worldview is identical to that of Slim Shady (remember, people did this. Quaint, huh? Probably not, if you were Mr. Mathers). Such readings are depressingly shallow. It ought to go without saying that a writer can explore scenes of unmitigated horror without endorsing their real life equivalents. And in most cases, the writer's outraged humanity is the fuel behind such explorations in the first place. If I hadn't been hurt in certain ways, my own scrutiny of our tenuous connections and adult sorrows alongside their roots in childhood trauma would probably ring hollow or skewed or inauthentic. Perhaps they do anyway. But, as

Stephen King so succinctly said once, "We make up horrors to help us cope with the real ones."

Yes, there is exploitation. Yes, there is insensitivity. Stupidity, even. Those are matters for the writer and his or her conscience. And for readers to embrace or shun as they see fit. But freedom of speech is essential to a democracy, and especially to our current very flawed versions. Without even that, freedom itself would only further adopt the worryingly illusory mantle it's already begun to.

Again, so I am not misunderstood: I'm not telling you what to do. As a writer, you might have your own (personal, religious, ethical) limits with regard to what topics you allow yourself to explore. That's fine. Some writers aim only to entertain, and I mean it, there's nothing wrong with that. I may disagree with what I see as misguided morality but I respect your right to it. But those of us who dig around in the entrails sometimes need to feel our discussion of the world's sharper edges or bleaker corners will not be interpreted as endorsement or approval of such horrors. I have always believed that art mirrors life and not the other way around. Those of us damaged by events in our personal lives (I'm hazarding a guess that's most of us) need this blighted avenue in which to explore our various wounds. Who knows, without that opportunity, and with only the misplaced appraisals of the misinformed and the judgmental, maybe more of us would end up being the Hannibal Lecters of the world instead of the Thomas Harris's.

Look, it's a lonely enough profession. I sometimes think I write to combat the loneliness more than for any other reason. It's an attempt to self heal. Okay, I just ran out of steam, so I'll end on another fairly pertinent quote by our old friend, Mr. King:

"Alone. Yes, that's the key word, the most awful word in the English tongue. Murder doesn't hold a candle to it and hell is only a poor synonym."

Chapter Twenty-Seven: Fear and Loathing No More

Long before the interwebs dubbed them "epic fails", I used to collect such stories in the dimly-lit, ironic laugh-a-thon I call my "mind". Like the bank robber who wrote his holdup note on the back of an envelope that not only displayed his own name and address clearly and almost heartbreakingly, but also that of his parole officer, upper left corner, return address. Then… *he left the envelope at the bank.* Or a different guy—surely related via some spectacular yet hitherto undiscovered boneheadedness gene—who held up the teller with a rifle… but left the cork plugged proudly and prominently in the end of his painfully-obvious-to-everyone toy firearm.

Anyway, that's a trip down Fail Boulevard. And highly amusing as that journey undoubtedly is, I want to explore another part of town: Success Street. Success. Even the word itself sounds like it tastes good (*cf:* succinct, succumb, succour, succulent). Yeah. Did I ever mention how much I love words? So much so I want to eat them. With bacon. And chocolate-dipped seahorse roe.

But I digress.

Look, without further ado, here are **seven awesome ways to totally guarantee your writing success**.

7. Whether you write fiction or nonfiction, insert the word "Game" in your title. It certainly worked for Orson Scott Card (Ender!), Clive Barker (Damnation!), Tom Clancy (Patriot!), George R. R. Martin (Thrones!), Neil Strauss (seduction!) and Suzanne Collins (Hunger!).

Although I suppose the jury's still out on Herman Hesse... not altogether surprising, given *The Glass Bead Game*'s so not-intimidating German title (*Das Glasperlenspiel*) as well as the novel's popular and frothy mix of existentialist, epistemological and ontological themes. Ahem. But the overall idea is sound. If it's not already taken, I suggest something like *The Hungry Game of Patriotic Seduction*. Kind of puts you in mind of a Clancy/Kundera collab. Which would be magnificent. Oh, and for your sequel, you might want a title that somehow incorporates girls with interesting tattoos and frustrated soccer moms just beginning to explore the pain/pleasure dichotomy.

6. Don't just make your vampires sparkly, make them iridescent. In fact, make them musical. So they walk into a room accompanied by the ominous baritone strains of "Bela Lugosi's Dead". Also, give them love interest. Try to avoid thinking about how skeevy they actually are, given their deathly pallor and propensity for amorous violations of the species barrier. Along these lines, make them handsome and/or beautiful so your readers completely overlook the fact they resemble something that died in its parents' basement a long time ago. Writing is stage(d) magic, right? As in, sleight-of-hand and misdirection. Readers are suckers. Just never say that last part again. Ever. Not even with your inside voice.

5. Worry about how your target audience will react to everything. Pander to them. Shy away from profanity, sex and violence, and assume your readership is as rigidly and deeply puritanical as a fingerwag of church ladies at a Calvinist Convention... in Alabama. Actually, forget that last one: violence is your birthright as an American. As the aforementioned George R. R. Martin aptly put it: "I can describe an axe entering a human skull in great explicit detail and no one will blink twice at it. I provide a similar description, just as detailed, of a penis entering a vagina, and I get letters about it and people swearing off. To my mind this is kind of frustrating, it's madness. Ultimately, in the history of [the] world, penises entering vaginas have given a lot of people a lot of pleasure; axes entering skulls, well, not so much."

4. Take a stand on the big publishing issues of the day and stick to your guns, even in the face of any contradictory evidence. No, wait: don't just stick to your effete, feeble Saturday night specials—amass bigger and better versions! Fully automatics. RPGs. Decide whether this issue is black. Or whether that one's white. Never grey, nuh-uh. I mean, really, how does one choose a specific shade of grey when they are essentially infinite (certainly more than a paltry *fifty*, Ms. E. L. James)? Simple: one doesn't. So, go ahead, decide that the traditional publishing houses are ancient, threatened elitists dripping with unctuous literary pretension or decide that independent authors are a talentless hollow-eyed Noob Army of wretched hacks who are to fine writing what Justin Bieber is to fine musicianship. But decide. And don't dare waver or show nuance. Nuance is just another word for "liberal pantywaist do-gooder", after all. No. Save "flexibility" for your special yoga moments.

3. Defend your brand. Your brand being you, obviously. If someone has the audacity to dislike one of your books in a review, take the fight to Amazon. Or beyond. Argue and defend it all over the interwebs. It's your baby. You are almost literally advocating for your kid at the most dysfunctional school board meeting you've ever attended. You need to make horrible threats, maybe even personalize the conflict by accusing your reviewer of ~~having a balloon animal fetish~~ trying to ruin you. Use every rhetorical trick in the book to belittle your attackers, pull no punches. How can you be the bully when you are one and they are many? Right? It's more important to demonstrate your passion than your professionalism. Just ask Gordon Ramsay.

2. Spam. I mean spam the living hell out of every Facebook group, every Twitter account, every Goodreads and LinkedIn group you can conceivably sign up for. Cover the online world with your bland, pink, lukewarm meat. Make sure you log in every day and repeat the same blurb about how your book is the bestest and most awesomest book since Stephen King and J. K. Rowling teamed up to invent rabid St Bernards who eat bespectacled young wizards in deserted Colorado hotels. Use multiple exclamation points. And don't make friends. They take up too much of your promo time.

1. Die. This is the most surefire yet simultaneously most drastic way to achieve success in the arts, and only recommended when all else fails. Actually, I don't really recommend it at all; it's generally a stupid idea and will make people cry. Unless you are already known for crazy. And even then, it's worth pointing out that what worked for Hunter S. Thompson may not work for the average person. This is a man whose body contained more drugs in his lifetime than all of Bristol-Myers Squibb and Pfizer combined, a man whose remains were fired out of a cannon to the tune of Norman Greenbaum's "Spirit in the Sky". I think it's safe to say his example was pretty much an outlier by any measure you could choose to make.

Chapter Twenty-Eight: Off the Hook

You've probably already heard that wonderfully creepy urban tale about a teenage boy and girl making out in a car in some Lovers Lane in Anytown, USA, and how the boy starts telling the girl of the "Hook Murders" in the area, whereby amorous teens are being killed by an insane, escaped killer with a hook for a hand. Perhaps not the smartest move on the boy's part, as his girlfriend gets all distracted by fear, going from initial anxiety to eventual near-hysteria, resisting his advances and demanding they leave *that instant*. Which he eventually does. He's all bummed, they bicker on the way back, arrive at her place, she jumps out, slams the door.... and screams. He runs around to her side of the vehicle.... and sees what she sees: a single bloody hook dangling from the door handle.

Creeped out? Good, because I am, and a good haunting is no fun alone.

So, already predisposed to think of hooks, I was struck by a thought the other day. This is by no means a common event, so I don't want to minimize its surprise value. Along the lines of Barry Eisler's recent advice on Indies Unlimited to read like a writer, I was considering opening lines—of both short fiction and longer—and how well they draw the reader in when skillfully crafted. But my mini epiphany occurred at the moment I realised an opening line isn't always a hook... although it probably should be. Certainly in shorter fiction. But even in a novel, you might really want to get your hook in no later than the first paragraph.

There are many forms available for your narrative hook, from similes and metaphors to character dilemmas and overt questions, even quotes and anecdotes. But the real world of books contains some incredible examples of opening hooks, thirty of which I'll now itemize here for your enjoyment (the numerical order isn't significant). Some are long and involved, although most are short and, at least on the surface, simply describe something essential to the story, without adornment or prevarication (yet don't let that fool you; some of these writers are wily foxes). I'll throw in the odd stray opinion as I go, usually as to why I find the words so damn compelling.

30. "The candleflame and the image of the candleflame caught in the pierglass twisted and righted when he entered the hall and again when he shut the door." — Cormac McCarthy, *All the Pretty Horses*

(This immediately alerts the reader to two things: McCarthy will invent compound words like there's no tomorrow, and the vision behind this is going to be both cinematic and literary.)

29. "As Gregor Samsa awoke one morning from uneasy dreams he found himself transformed in his bed into a gigantic insect." — Franz Kafka, *Metamorphosis*

(Sounds almost like a children's fable, doesn't it? Uh, keep reading. Which you almost can't help doing after reading that particular opener. Which is the point.)

28. "Far out in the uncharted backwaters of the unfashionable end of the Western Spiral arm of the Galaxy lies a small unregarded yellow sun." — Douglas Adams, *The Hitchhiker's Guide to the Galaxy*

(With one word, "unfashionable", Adams transforms this opener from potential mundanity into something richly comedic. After which he seals the deal by almost casually throwing in "unregarded".)

27. "Mrs. Dalloway said she would buy the flowers herself." — Virginia Woolf, *Mrs. Dalloway*

(I have to admit, some of these opening lines take on incredible poignancy and significance in hindsight, via an almost insane level of initial understatement.)

26. "They murdered him." — Robert Cormier, *The Chocolate War*

(I love it when someone cuts right to the chase. Or does he? He actually gives us almost nothing. Who is the victim? Who are "they"? We simply have to read on.)

25. "It was the day my grandmother exploded." — Iain Banks, *The Crow Road*

(Um. Okay. Intriguing, you have to say. And who, aside from volatile, unstable grandmothers, won't read on?)

24. "Call me Ishmael." — Herman Melville, *Moby-Dick*

(Again, simple. But why *call me* Ishmael? Is that not the protagonist's name? If it were, he'd surely have written, "My name is Ishmael." What trickery is afoot here? Oh, and yes, the novel's title really is hyphenated, I Googled.)

23. "Like the brief doomed flare of exploding suns that registers dimly on blind men's eyes, the beginning of the horror passed almost unnoticed; in the shriek of what followed, in fact, was forgotten and perhaps not connected to the horror at all." — William Peter Blatty, *The Exorcist*

(Well, I got chills.)

22. "We were somewhere around Barstow on the edge of the desert when the drugs began to take hold." — Hunter S. Thompson, *Fear and Loathing in Las Vegas*

(Could be another example of an opening line taking on all the subsequent cultural baggage unleashed not simply by the book itself, but by the movie adaptations and HST's real life exploits. Still good, though.)

21. "On my naming day when I come 12 I gone front spear and kilt a wyld boar he parbly ben the las wyld pig on the Bundel Downs any how there hadnt ben none for a long time befor him nor I aint looking to see none agen." — Russell Hoban, *Riddley Walker*

(One of my personal favourites. Post-apocalyptic and primitivist, another coming-of-age fable for grown up children. You know he's gonna make you work but if you can grok these opening words even a little, you know the rewards will be there for you.)

20. "Tyler gets me a job as a waiter, after that Tyler's pushing a gun in my mouth and saying, the first step to eternal life is you have to die." — Chuck Palahniuk, *Fight Club*

(Well, if you love words and storytelling, you just can't fault that as an opener, can you?)

19. "In the beginning, God created the heavens and the earth." — Genesis, *The Holy Bible*

(Well, duh. They sound pretty sure of that. No pyrotechnics, though. And, given the stakes, probably the most understated opening line ever.)

18. "Dog carcass in alley this morning, tire tread on burst stomach. This city is afraid of me. I have seen its true face." — Alan Moore and Dave Gibbons, *Watchmen*

(Yeah, it's a graphic novel, and some of the impact is lost without Gibbons' artwork, but it's still an evocative opener.)

17. "The great grey beast February had eaten Harvey Swick alive." — Clive Barker, *The Thief of Always*

(Elusive and allusive, Barker's technique alone will make me read on, even without such a startling metaphor.)

16. "A screaming comes across the sky." — Thomas Pynchon, *Gravity's Rainbow*

(It grabs you in a visceral way, for sure, and it also becomes much clearer as you read on. I do lean toward the succinct openers, it seems. There's no real warning here of the approaching complexities of Pynchon's prose. Or even that he's making a lame sexual pun.)

15. "The man in black fled across the desert, and the gunslinger followed." — Stephen King, *The Dark Tower: The Gunslinger*

(Not only simple, rhythmically pleasing, cinematic even, but it points to something later on that I won't elaborate on for fear of spoilers. Just read this series, is all I can say, and this line will return to haunt you, again and again.)

14. "No live organism can continue for long to exist sanely under conditions of absolute reality; even larks and katydids are supposed, by some, to dream. Hill House, not sane, stood by itself against its hills, holding darkness within; it had stood so for eighty years and might stand for eighty more. Within, walls continued upright, bricks met neatly, floors were firm, and doors were sensibly shut; silence lay steadily against the wood and stone of Hill House, and whatever walked there, walked alone." — Shirley Jackson, *The Haunting of Hill House*

(And here's the exception to my general preference for short and pithy. This is fine writing. And creepy as hell. Those of you reading these chapters in order might even recognize this from an earlier discussion of closing lines. Oh, that "not sane" gets me every time.)

13. "Imagine a ruin so strange it must never have happened." — Barbara Kingsolver, *The Poisonwood Bible*

(I love this. If you haven't read this novel, please let the airy, expectant poetry of this opener convince you to do so. And what an audacious line to use in a fictional work.)

12. "When he was nearly thirteen, my brother Jem got his arm badly broken at the elbow." — Harper Lee, *To Kill a Mockingbird*

(Again, this contains information that is essential, but it doesn't even begin to scratch the surface of the events behind it. A badly broken elbow may in itself seem a weighty topic to such a very young narrator, but… yeah, read on.)

11. "Mother died today. Or, maybe, yesterday; I can't be sure." — Albert Camus, *The Stranger*

(Okay. In the merest handful of words, Camus suggests dislocation, dissociation and indifference, or some awful combination of them all. If you don't want to read on from here, your curiosity engine must have seized on you.)

10. "In a hole in the ground there lived a hobbit." — J. R. R. Tolkien, *The Hobbit*

(Up there with the damn Bible, in its way. What the hell is a hobbit? Did he just misspell "rabbit?" Oh, he's a wily one, he knows exactly what you're thinking.)

9. "It can hardly be a coincidence that no language on earth has ever produced the expression 'As pretty as an airport.'" — Douglas Adams, *The Long Dark Tea-Time of the Soul*

(Ha! When in doubt, crack your audience up from the get-go. Dry, sardonic, just very funny, even the title itself.)

8. "The sky above the port was the colour of television, tuned to a dead channel." — William Gibson, *Neuromancer*

(Perfect use of metaphor, and so apt in a book that had such a huge influence on the *Matrix* movies.)

7. "It was a bright cold day in April, and the clocks were striking thirteen." — George Orwell, *Nineteen Eighty-Four*

(It's all about that "thirteen", isn't it? I mean, wha—? This guy got a thing about numbers?)

6. "When he woke in the woods in the dark and the cold of the night he'd reach out to touch the child sleeping beside him." — Cormac McCarthy, *The Road*

(Again, more poignant in retrospect, but very much in keeping with the quietly relentless monochrome tone of the rest of the novel. That seed of love is there in the very first sentence. Carrying the fire.)

5. "All this happened, more or less." — Kurt Vonnegut, *Slaughterhouse-Five*

(Thanks Kurt. So did it or didn't it? Now we must find out, you sly dog, you.)

4. "First of all, it was October, a rare month for boys." — Ray Bradbury, *Something Wicked This Way Comes*

(Brilliant. Making "first" literally the first word, it's almost a step on from "once upon a time". And again, plenty of information in so few words.)

3. "I did not kill my father, but I sometimes felt I had helped him on his way." — Ian McEwan, *The Cement Garden*

(This is a remarkably accomplished novel considering it was McEwan's debut, and this line shows all the assurance that, as a pure technician, he's never relinquished.)

2. "Context is everything. Dress me up and see. I'm a carnival barker, an auctioneer, a downtown performance artist, a speaker in tongues, a senator drunk on filibuster." — Jonathan Lethem, *Motherless Brooklyn*

(This is intriguing enough… and then you get to the very next line, which is italicized, and it's like the sun emerges from behind a cloud. Context, indeed. Wanna know what it is? Nah, not telling. Read it.)

1. "Ten thousand bombs had landed, and I was waiting for George." — Rawi Hage, *DeNiro's Game*

(I like this juxtaposition of the ordinary with the apparently extraordinary. This is a very beautifully written novel, incidentally.)

Oh, and speaking of strange juxtapositions, here's a bonus pair:

"It is a truth universally acknowledged, that a single man in possession of a good fortune must be in want of a wife." — Jane Austen, *Pride and Prejudice*

"It is a truth universally acknowledged that a zombie in possession of brains must be in want of more brains." — Jane Austen and Seth Grahame-Smith, *Pride and Prejudice and Zombies*

Chapter Twenty-Nine: The Uber Cannons of Snark

Okay, I'm going to go full douchenozzle in this post. You may know me for, and gotten used to, my mildly snarky yet oddly gentle sense of humour, but enough's enough. Time on this occasion to unleash both barrels of **The Über Cannons of Snark**.

No messing about, here are eight dick moves for writers, and once you've read them, please stop doing them. Now. And I'm turning the barrels on myself, too: I've been as guilty as anyone with a few of these. Well, a couple, at least. Okay, one of them.

8. Quit trying to earn your book nerd cred. Telling people you don't own a television and that you don't even miss it doesn't actually make you look the erudite techno-rebel you think it does. Or the noble ascetic, either. Or whatever other worthy character your inner movie is projecting on the murky screen inside your head. No, it makes you look more like an elitist luddite and an extremist bizarropod. Guess what, folks? You can own and even occasionally watch a television and you might on occasion be entertained or learn something or catch a great *Seinfeld* rerun or discover how badass the honey badger really is (wait, that's YouTube) or marvel at Lionel Messi's close ball control or weep uncontrollably at an old classic movie… or at Mitt Romney's awkward and obvious avoidance of any questions with the letters T, A and X in close proximity… and none of this will prevent you from also reading books. One does not exclude the other. May I repeat that? *One does not exclude the other!* Blaming TV for all the pop culture trash out there is like blaming the internet for porn… oh wait…. Think I broke my brain again. Give me a second…

7. Speaking of pop culture trash, bemoaning the fact Snooki has a bestselling book to her name does nothing for you other than to raise your blood pressure a few notches. It's stupid and pointless. As, indeed, you believe the young lady herself to be. But let's reframe it: she is an example of a young person from a generation many older folk dismiss as unmotivated and entitled. Did she sit around in various bars and clubs in Seaside Heights getting hella crunk like you assume most of her contemporaries did/do? Well, okay, sort of. But the key is, *she did it on camera*, even getting *punched in the face* for her troubles, and did it all with enough tawdry poignance that people couldn't help but notice her. And try watching the scene where she's so achingly (and at that point, pretty much deservedly) lonely she wanders the boardwalk barefoot, literally begging for someone to party with her, without feeling even a twinge of genuine pity in your black and empty heart. Just try it. Anyway, she bootstrapped her decidedly odd and needy defiance into something lucrative. Fair play to her. So what? Move on, that's what.

6. In fact, stop being envious, period. Of sparkly vampires or soccer mom spanking sessions. Lamenting your own obscurity while publicly calling out examples of undeserved success is not a good look. Who gets to decide the "undeserved" part? Do you really want to end up looking like those hoary old classic rock bands in the '70s who turned up their noses at upstarts like… the Sex Pistols? The Clash? The Ramones? Again, we don't have to take sides, we can listen to *both*, capiche? Even if we're a dinosaur (and at some point, everyone has to take his or her turn in the Dino-dome), it's better to be

Neil Young than Ted fucking Nugent, after all. And I'm not even saying that because I'm Canadian; it's just obvious: Neil is still awesome and Nugent is an utter asswipe. It's a no-brainer. Anyway. Embrace it all and stop experiencing life in narrowcast (or something… sometimes I worry even *I* don't know what I'm talking about). And when it comes to music, thanks partly to the whole iTunes revolution, we seem to have collectively gotten that message at last. Now we just need to extend it to books and realize how much of this is simply down to subjective taste and stop reinventing hierarchies that only ever succeed in pissing everyone off or, worse, intimidating new writers into quitting before they've ever had the chance to learn and hone their skills. Stop telling people who's allowed to eat at the big folks' table. Besides, the big folks' table looks a little dull. And you can't even put your elbows on it.

5. Oh, and the corollary to that last one: if you do begin to experience a measure of success, be gracious about it. Don't set odd little traps for others. Don't suddenly act like the King or Queen of *I Am Bearer Of The Ultimate Secret* and start rubbing your friends' faces in it only to then turn around and imply they're acting jealous when in fact they're only being aghast and uncomfortable at your embarrassing hubris. No, this is bad behaviour all around, stop it. Sure, success can be down to hard work, but there's often a measure of sheer random luck involved, right-place-right-time kind of thing. Many writers work their typing fingers to the calcium-depleted bone with relatively little success. You gonna tell them they don't deserve it? Some of them? All of them? And even more pertinent: you cannot know whether this relative upsurge in your own fortunes will last. What is that thing they say pride comes before? You know exactly what I'm saying. Show a little humility, fool. Be kind.

4. Back in the day, writers were sticklike figures barely subsisting on the rotted cotton wadding inside an old stained recliner they dragged to their meagre garret from an alleyway before the rats could use it for nests. They were isolated and flea-bitten wrecks, drinking methylated spirits until blindness finally destroyed their only chance at literary fame and fortune. Okay, not really, them's stereotypes, but indulge me. In place of unbearable loneliness, we now have…. Facebook. Social media. Which we're told to use relentlessly, to connect with people like a string of special and—thanks to inactivity and the universal accessibility of Cheetos—increasingly odd-shaped snowflakes. Snowflakes with orange teeth. And we do it. We even befriend people, genuinely. It's a social thing. We're a social animal. The artificial divide between writer and reader is now virtually gone (sorry, pun not intended). Which is great and everything, but now we can bite back… snipe back directly at the suddenly malicious critics and readers who attack our precious babies. We can use the very tools we're most adept in—words—to strike, like Jules Winnfield, with great vengeance and furious anger on our foes. Everywhere. On Amazon. On our personal blogs. On Facebook. Twitter. Mwahahaha, we are The Forgers of Words, hear us roar… Well, no. We really shouldn't do that. Not even once. It will have no effect other than to convince a sizeable number of silent observers that we're an arsey little hosebag. And, wherever you are posting or commenting on the interwebs, never forget the vast, silent bank of lurkers. Their eyes are beady and mean and they will watch you and they will judge you. It's sheer professional suicide to act like a handicapped badger's spleen… and besides, you know that hella cool "lay my vengeance upon thee" Ezekiel-schtick in *Pulp Fiction?* Tarantino made it the hell up. 'Nuff said.

3. Now, with this one I don't fully see eye to eye with many of my writer peers. I'm talking about politics and religion. And unlike others, I don't think you should avoid these topics. In fact, they're pretty much the motherlode for any discussion of the human condition, the sacred and the profane… which is what we as writers should be eating for breakfast. Before moving onto philosophy and existential eel porn by lunch time. So don't avoid them. But… *be tactful.* If someone disagrees with you, try not to call him a rabid baboon's esophagus. Quite honestly, the only writers I would advise to STFU on this stuff are the true bigots: the racists, the sexists, the homophobes. They just need to sit down, be quiet, watch how normal people work, and learn how utterly futile their pathetic attempts to swim against the prevailing winds are, almost as excruciatingly failworthy as my last metaphor, in fact.

2. Spam. You just knew the pink, lukewarm meat of doom was going to make an appearance, didn't you? Look, I get it. We're told, exhorted in fact, to promote our work across a kajillion social networks with names like Tinglr and GoodFellas and FaceSpace. So we sign up for most of them and then… we go nuts. This isn't one can of Spam, oh no, this is a cloying, gelatinous, somehow horribly sluggish, pink *slough* of the stuff. For the love of all that is holy, calm down. Breathe. Okay. You're in a vast hall, and there are small groups of people scattered around. First, you don't stand in the middle and randomly start yelling "Guys, I'm so excited! Got a 5-Star review on Smashwords today. Squeeee." Right? (In fact, please don't ever say *squee,* period, okay? Unless you're five and like to wear tiaras.) You certainly don't shoulder your way into a group and say, "I just sold three copies of my book on the Lithuanian version of Amazon this week!" No, you find a conversation that interests you, and you politely join in when there's a lull. It's really that simple. Do the stuff yo' mama taught you. Check you don't have spinach in your teeth. Wash behind your ears. Say please and thank you. Don't interrupt. Don't fart and blame it on the server. Be nice. And guess what? People will like you. After which, there may come a time when someone turns to you and asks, "so what is it you do?" Bingo! The online world really is but a reflection of the real world... only with way more kitties... and lots more naughty stuff. But yeah, it's common sense, really. Moderation. Balance. If you feel you've crossed the line this week, cool your jets next week.

1. I was going to talk about dodgy or questionable ethics surrounding the whole recent reviews controversy, but I think I'm going to leave that to someone who will do it far more justice than I ever could here. Instead, I'll end somewhat anticlimactically on a subject that will make most of you sigh and look at your watch and say, "oh, is that the time?" Namely... editing. Yes, go ahead, scurry away, you horrible little wordworm, but you know what's coming, don't you? I can still see you, so Imma shout at your retreating backs: "HIRE AN EDITOR!" Now, this final item is in no way self-serving (cough, http://www.bewritethere.com, hack), but it cannot and should not be avoided. If money's tight, go the beta reader route... something. Can you imagine if God himself had thought "You know, in the time it'll take me to find an editor, I could have this thing up and running and put through Coker's meatgrinder twice over, and besides, I think I'm a pretty good writer, possibly even

135

the best, certainly the first. Nah, forget it, who'll even know"? You might have gotten something like this:

1. At the start, God made up heaven and earth.

2. And teh earth was without from, and void; and drakness was up all over the face of the deep. And the Spirit of God moved upon the face of teh waters.

3. And God says, Let their be light: and thurr was light.

4. And God seen the light, that it was a'ight: and God partitioned the light from teh darkness.

5. And God called the light Day, and the darkness he thought about for a bit and eventually decided to call Night.

6. And the evening and the mourning were the 1st day.

Wait, the evening was the first *day?* Um… help? Someone? Where'd that goddamned editor go?

Outro

That's it. We're done. If you like any of my inane ruminations, my insouciant lack of any real style, or even the overall cut of my jib, feel free to seek me out on the worldwide interwebs. I have written other things in other guises, and although my first book (*Dissolute Kinship: A 9/11 Road Trip*) is also a nonfiction memoir (of sorts), my large, wounded heart beats more frequently to a kind of lyrical, surreal, speculative fiction. Think Lynch crossed with Barker. To that end, I have stories in various anthologies and you might want to look out for my (as yet untitled) forthcoming collection of creepy, horror-inflected tales.

Oh, and my website/blog is called The Migrant Type (http://www.the-migrant-type.com) and if you show up and comment, I will happily talk to you, as I have no friends.